W9-AJN-090

BAPTISTWAYPRESS®

Adult Bible Study Guide

Psalms and Proverbs

Songs and Sayings of Faith

Mike Smith
Ron Lyles
Bob Campbell

BAPTISTWAYPRESS®
Dallas, Texas

Psalms and Proverbs: Songs and Sayings of Faith—
Adult Bible Study Guide—Large Print
Copyright © 2006 by BAPTISTWAY PRESS®.
All rights reserved.
Printed in the United States of America.

No part of this book may be used or reproduced in any manner whatsoever without written permission except in the case of brief quotations. For information, contact BAPTISTWAY PRESS, Baptist General Convention of Texas, 333 North Washington, Dallas, TX 75246–1798.

BAPTISTWAY PRESS® is registered in U.S. Patent and Trademark Office.

Scripture marked NIV is taken from The Holy Bible, New International Version (North American Edition), copyright © 1973, 1978, 1984 by the International Bible Society. Used by permission of Zondervan Publishing House. Unless otherwise indicated, all Scripture quotations in the *Study Guide* materials on Psalms and Proverbs are from the New International Version.

Scripture marked NASB is taken from the New American Standard Bible®, Copyright © The Lockman Foundation 1960, 1962, 1963, 1968, 1971, 1972, 1973, 1975, 1977, 1995. Used by permission.

Scripture marked NRSV is taken from the New Revised Standard Version Bible, copyright 1989, Division of Christian Education of the National Council of the Churches of Christ in the United States of America. Used by permission. All rights reserved.

BAPTISTWAY PRESS® Management Team
Executive Director, Baptist General Convention of Texas: Charles Wade
Director, Missions, Evangelism, and Ministry Team: Wayne Shuffield
Ministry Team Leader: Phil Miller

Editor & publishing consultant: Ross West, Positive Difference Communications
Cover and Interior Design and Production: Desktop Miracles, Inc.
Printing: Data Reproductions Corporation
Cover Photo: Mount Hermon (Psalm 42:6), www.istockphoto.com

First edition: September 2006
ISBN: 1–931060–80–0

How to Make the Best Use of This Issue

Whether you're the teacher or a student—

1. Start early in the week before your class meets.
2. Overview the study. Review the table of contents and read the study introduction. Try to see how each lesson relates to the overall study.
3. Use your Bible to read and consider prayerfully the Scripture passages for the lesson. (You'll see that each writer has chosen a favorite translation for the lessons in this issue. You're free to use the Bible translation you prefer and compare it with the translation chosen for that unit, of course.)
4. After reading all the Scripture passages in your Bible, then read the writer's comments. The comments are intended to be an aid to your study of the Bible.
5. Read the small articles—"sidebars"—in each lesson. They are intended to provide additional, enrichment information and inspiration and to encourage thought and application.
6. Try to answer for yourself the questions included in each lesson. They're intended to encourage further thought and application, and they can also be used in the class session itself.

If you're the teacher—

A. Do all of the things just mentioned, of course. In the first session of the study, briefly overview the study by identifying with your class the date on which each lesson will be studied. Lead your class to write the date in the table of contents on page 7 and on the first page of each lesson. You might also find it helpful to make and post a chart that indicates the date on which each lesson will be studied. If all of your class has e-mail, send them an e-mail with the dates the lessons will be studied. (At least one church that uses BAPTISTWAY® materials for its classes places a sticker on the table of contents to identify the dates.)
B. Get a copy of the *Teaching Guide*, a companion piece to this *Study Guide*. The *Teaching Guide* contains additional Bible comments plus two teaching plans. The teaching plans in the *Teaching Guide* are intended to provide practical, easy-to-use teaching suggestions that will work in your class.
C. After you've studied the Bible passage, the lesson comments, and other material, use the teaching suggestions in the *Teaching Guide* to help you develop your plan for leading your class in studying each lesson.
D. You may want to get the additional adult Bible study comments—*Adult Online Bible*

Commentary—by Dr. Jim Denison, pastor of Park Cities Baptist Church, Dallas, Texas, that are available at www.baptistwaypress.org and can be downloaded free. An additional teaching plan plus teaching resource items are also available at www.baptistwaypress.org.

E. You also may want to get the enrichment teaching help that is provided on the internet by the *Baptist Standard* at www.baptiststandard.com. (Other class participants may find this information helpful, too.) Call 214–630–4571 to begin your subscription to the printed edition of the *Baptist Standard.*

F. Enjoy leading your class in discovering the meaning of the Scripture passages and in applying these passages to their lives.

Psalms and Proverbs: Songs and Sayings of Faith

THE BOOK OF PSALMS

Songs of Faith

Psalms and Proverbs: *Songs and Sayings of Faith*

THE BOOK OF PROVERBS

Sayings of Faith

Writers of This Study Guide

Mike Smith wrote lessons 1–4 on Psalms. Dr. Smith is pastor of First Baptist Church, Murfreesboro, Tennessee. He formerly was pastor of other churches in Tennessee, Kentucky, and Indiana. He has served as president of the executive board of the Tennessee Baptist Convention and on the coordinating council of the Cooperative Baptist Fellowship. He is a graduate of Belmont University and The Southern Baptist Theological Seminary (Ph.D.).

Ron Lyles, pastor of South Main Baptist Church, Pasadena, Texas, wrote lessons 5–9 on Psalms. Dr. Lyles is a graduate of Dallas Baptist University and Southwestern Baptist Theological Seminary (M. Div., Ph.D.). He has taught adjunctively for Houston Baptist University and for the Logsdon School of Theology.

Bob Campbell wrote the lessons on Proverbs. He is retired after forty-seven years of ministry. He last served as pastor of Westbury Baptist Church, Houston, Texas. In addition to other pastorates, Dr. Campbell was professor of Bible at Howard Payne University, Brownwood, Texas. He served as president of the Baptist General Convention of Texas. He is a graduate of Louisiana College and Southwestern Baptist Theological Seminary (B.D., Th.D.).

Introducing

The Book of Psalms: Songs of Faith

The Book of Psalms may well be the most read and most influential book in the Old Testament. It has been used by God's people through the ages both to sing praises to God and to hear God's message to them. So, as we study this book, we join a vast company of believers who have been blessed by it. Too, let us keep in mind both uses for the Book of Psalms—to sing praises to God and to hear God's message.

The Psalms—God's Message to Us

The Book of Psalms has indeed been the hymnbook of God's people. That began with its use in temple worship in Old Testament days, and it extended into use in worship by the early church (see Ephesians 5:19; Colossians 3:16) and in later church history. In fact, for close to two hundred years after the Reformation in the sixteenth century, only the psalms, and not what we would call hymns, were used in worship in many churches.

Even more than being the hymnbook of God's people, though, the Book of Psalms is God's message to God's people. That is the spirit in which we will study the Book of Psalms in these Bible study lessons. Although the psalms are couched in the language of people's praises and pleas to God, they are God's message to us. As we read and study the psalms, let us listen and learn.

Approaching the Psalms

Obviously, with 150 psalms, we will study only a few of them in this series of nine lessons. So how shall we approach the study of the book? Several possibilities come to mind.

First, we could study selected psalms that have meant much to the devotional life of Christians, psalms like Psalm 23. We would seek mainly to apply them devotionally.

Or, second, we could study selected psalms on specific subjects. One of the achievements of scholarly study of the Book of Psalms in the twentieth century was the classification of the various psalms according to literary type. The leader in this effort was an Old Testament scholar named Hermann Gunkel. As he studied and compared the psalms, he noticed particularly their vocabulary and structure and the feelings that seemed to arise from various psalms. As a result, he described five major types of psalms.[1] The major literary types identified were as follows: (1) hymns of praise to God; (2) community laments, calling for help for the community as a whole; (3) individual laments, in which an individual pleads for God's help; (4) psalms of individual thanksgiving; (5) royal psalms, meaning psalms related to the king. Some of these types have sub-categories within them. Too, in addition to these five major types are seven minor types. Among these minor types are wisdom psalms, creation psalms, and enthronement psalms. The identification of these types has been helpful, and other Bible students have built on these classifications, refined them, and also adjusted them in various ways. This approach of studying the Psalms according to their literary types has much to commend it as a way of gaining a fuller understanding of these 150 psalms.

Yet another possibility is to pay attention to the divisions within the Book of Psalms itself and to consider how the psalms are arranged into five books within the Book of Psalms. These books are identified in the text of the Book of Psalms as Book I (Psalms 1—41; see Ps. 1); Book II (Psalms 42—72; see Ps. 42); Book III (Psalms 73—89; see Ps. 73); Book IV (Psalms 90—106; see Ps. 90); and Book V (Psalms 107—150; see Ps. 107).

Rather than choosing from among these approaches, we will take note of all three.[2] That is, we will study some of the choicest, most revered, and most memorable psalms. Too, in choosing the psalms to study, we have chosen psalms within most of the major categories Bible students have identified. In addition, we will organize the study so as to move through the five books within the Book of Psalms.

God Speaking Through the Psalms

One thing we can readily see as we read and study the Book of Psalms is that these psalms speak of a deeply personal and meaningful faith. The psalmists did not hold faith at arms' length. Rather, they embraced it. As we listen to God speaking to us through the psalms, may we let ourselves be embraced by God, and may we embrace God in return.[3]

THE BOOK OF PSALMS: SONGS OF FAITH

Lesson 1	The Way to True Happiness	Psalm 1
Lesson 2	Pleading for God's Help	Psalms 3; 13; 22:1–5, 22–24
Lesson 3	Trusting in a Caring God	Psalms 23; 27:1–6
Lesson 4	Thirsting for God	Psalms 42—43
Lesson 5	Almost Doubting	Psalm 73
Lesson 6	The Joy of Worshiping God Together	Psalm 84
Lesson 7	To Live a Life That Matters	Psalm 90
Lesson 8	Praise for God's Goodness	Psalms 100; 103
Lesson 9	Give Thanks for God's Blessings	Psalm 116

Additional Resources for Studying the Book of Psalms[4]

W. H. Bellinger, Jr. *Psalms: Reading and Studying the Book of Praises.* Peabody, Massachusetts: Hendrickson Publishers, 1990.

W. H. Bellinger, Jr. *The Testimony of Poets and Sages: The Psalms and Wisdom Literature.* Macon, Georgia: Smyth and Helwys Publishing, Inc., 1997.

Nancy L. deClaissé-Walford. *Introduction to the Psalms: A Song from Ancient Israel.* St. Louis, Missouri: Chalice Press, 2004.

Nancy L. deClaissé-Walford. *Reading from the Beginning: The Shaping of the Hebrew Psalter.* Macon, Georgia: Mercer University Press, 1997.

John I. Durham, "Psalms," *The Broadman Bible Commentary.* Volume 4. Nashville, Tennessee: Broadman Press, 1971.

J. Clinton McCann, Jr. "Psalms." *The New Interpreter's Bible.* Volume 4. Nashville: Abingdon Press, 1996.

James Luther Mays. *Psalms.* Interpretation: A Bible Commentary for Teaching and Preaching. Louisville, Kentucky: John Knox Press, 1994.

Marvin E. Tate. *Psalms 51—100.* Word Biblical Commentary. Waco, Texas: Word, 1990.

NOTES

1. See W. H. Bellinger, Jr., *The Testimony of Poets and Sages: The Psalms and Wisdom Literature* (Macon, Georgia: Smyth and Helwys Publishing, Inc., 1997), 10–12; and Nancy L. deClaissé-Walford, *Introduction to the Psalms: A Song from Ancient Israel* (St. Louis, Missouri: Chalice Press, 2004), 20–27.
2. A fourth approach might be to study the various collections within the Book of Psalms, such as, among others, the Davidic collection (3—41; 51—72; 138—145); the Korahite collection (42—49; 84–85; 87—88); the Asaphite collection (73—83); or the song of ascents collection (120—134). Note the superscriptions of the psalms in these particular collections. See deClaissé-Walford, *Introduction to the Psalms*, 35–40.
3. Unless otherwise indicated, all Scripture quotations in this article, "Introducing the Book of Psalms: Songs of Faith," and the lessons on Psalms are from the New International Version.
4. Listing a book does not imply full agreement by the writers or BAPTISTWAY PRESS® with all of its comments.

Focal Text

Psalm 1

Background

Psalm 1

Main Idea

Following God faithfully leads to a full and happy life.

Question to Explore

What kind of life leads to true happiness?

LESSON ONE

The Way to True Happiness

Study Aim

To identify what true happiness is and how to experience it

Study and Action Emphases

- Affirm the Bible as our authoritative guide for life and ministry
- Share the gospel with all people
- Develop a growing, vibrant faith

Quick Read

If we want to build a fulfilled life, we must learn to follow God faithfully. Psalm 1 steers us away from dangerous detours and toward the right path.

When I reflect on Psalm 1, I find it useful to start with a mental exercise. Take the opening phrase—*Blessed is the person who. . . .* Then complete it as if no one would ever see the result. Be honest!

Once, while leading a small group in a study of Psalms, I challenged the participants to write their answers on small slips of paper. We dropped their answers into a hat and drew them out one by one. Some of the responses included the following:

Blessed is the person

- who strikes it rich
- who marries the prince or princess
- whose family members never go astray
- who gets elected
- who never loses a job
- who has great abs
- who has a boyfriend or girlfriend

We laughed aloud. After we settled down, one member of the group said, "It looks as if there's some distance between where we are and where the psalmist believes we should go." The next few hours of discussion focused on closing the gap. We talked about what to avoid, what to embrace, and the consequences.

Psalm 1

1 Blessed is the man
who does not walk in the counsel of the wicked

or stand in the way of sinners
  or sit in the seat of mockers.
2 But his delight is in the law of the LORD,
  and on his law he meditates day and night.
3 He is like a tree planted by streams of water,
  which yields its fruit in season
and whose leaf does not wither.
  Whatever he does prospers.
4 Not so the wicked!
  They are like chaff
that the wind blows away.
5 Therefore the wicked will not stand in the
    judgment,
  nor sinners in the assembly of the righteous.
6 For the LORD watches over the way of the righteous,
  but the way of the wicked will perish.

Take Care! (1:1)

The 150 psalms found in our Bible are organized into five sections or books. Psalm 1 is found in the first book and serves as a prelude or call to worship. Most scholars label Psalm 1 a *wisdom psalm*. Other wisdom psalms include Psalms 37, 49, 73, 112, 119, 127, 128, and 133. Wisdom psalms usually contrast the lives of the wise and foolish or the wicked and the righteous. They call us to practice discernment by recognizing and fleeing from ungodly counsel and embracing instead the counsel of God.

Psalm 1 teaches that those who choose to delight in the ways of God will be "blessed." Some translations use the term "happy" (NRSV). Either translation is acceptable, provided we remain open to learning how the psalmist defined the term.

The psalmist used three words to describe various kinds of ungodly counselors: "wicked," "sinners," and "mockers." As is often true of Hebrew poetry, the terms build on one another to strengthen the impact of the writer's message.

"It looks as if there's some distance between where we are and where the psalmist believes we should go."

"Wicked" is the most general of the terms and most likely refers to people whose personal conduct runs contrary to God's law or ways. The literal meaning of the Hebrew term is *unrest.* The wicked are those whose hearts are restless because they are out of touch with God. Not knowing what else to do, they seek direction and comfort in whatever comes to hand. They cannot offer good advice for living, for they do not know the way to genuine happiness. In effect the "wicked" say, *I don't know where I am going or where I've been, and I'm not overly certain as to where I am now—but you're welcome to come along with me.* A wise person refuses such an invitation.

The term translated "sinners" introduces a darker theme: the danger of taking counsel from those who knowingly and habitually depart from the law of God. "Sinners," at least at first, know what they are doing.

In essence, they say, *I know God's way calls me to practice honesty, but I choose to do otherwise.* Over time such choices become a way of life, a habit.

"Sinners" may actually come to believe their habits to be the real secrets to a happy life. I once knew a woman who grew up in the church and knew the ways of God. Due to a variety of experiences, she became bitter. She had been taught that God called his people to practice generosity toward those in need, but now she rejected such a way of life. She hoarded her money and thought others foolish when they contributed to various charitable endeavors. Going further, she actively tried to persuade her friends to embrace her perspective. The psalmist called on his readers to be wary of such people and to refuse to buy into their worldview.

Ungodly counsel often arrives in stealth mode.

"Mockers" may also be translated as *the scornful* or *scoffers.* At best they doubt the relevance of God, and some may even deny God's existence. When they encounter the law of God or someone concerned to embrace the ways of God, they respond with cynicism.

Note the terms "walk," "stand," and "sit." Commentators differ over their precise interpretation. The psalmist stacks the words in order to drive home his point: *Exercise great care lest you succumb to the lure of ungodly counselors and even join their ranks.* How might such a thing happen? Many years ago a Christian young man I knew well became addicted to a variety of hard drugs. The group of friends with whom he spent his time had suggested he try drugs and even supplied the first fixes. Soon the young man backed away from the church and began to steal in order to support his drug habit. When confronted, he parroted the arguments of his friends, insisting that hard drugs would not harm him. No matter how much we might wish it were not so, we generally assume the beliefs and practices of the people to whom we give our time.

The secret lay in his delight in and meditation on the ways of God.

Unfortunately, matters are not always so clear-cut. Ungodly counsel often arrives in stealth mode. Sometimes family members, broader culture, and even some forms of religion peddle bad advice. More often than not, people and institutions introduce us to racial prejudice, cynicism, distrust of God and others, runaway consumerism, self-loathing, and the like. Knowing whom to trust would be much simpler if the ungodly wore name tags or even placards that said, *Warning, I give bad advice!* The psalmist, therefore, urged us to be on guard.

Focus On God's Way (1:2)

The best way to build a blessed life is to focus on "the law of the LORD." The psalmist did not propose a set of techniques. Instead he urged us to take "delight" in the law of the Lord and to meditate on it.

What is "the law of the LORD"? Modern Christians often think first of the Ten Commandments. Some may also think of Leviticus. The psalmist probably meant something broader. "Law" translates the Hebrew term *torah*, which means teaching or direction. God's ancient people also called the first five books of the Old Testament *torah*. The sages or wise men of ancient Israel usually included proverbs (both the biblical book and assorted proverbs) and the like under the umbrella of *torah*. The psalmist taught that the blessed person centers his or her life on the things of God.

Can we imagine such a person? I find it easy to do so, for I've known a few such focused men and women. My maternal grandfather read his Bible each night. Hampered by an incomplete education, he read slowly. He often underlined passages that challenged or comforted him, and he wrote notes on the margins and on a pad of paper he kept with his Bible. After he had finished, my grandfather closed his eyes. When I was a small boy, I teasingly accused him of having fallen asleep. Actually, he used the time to pray and reflect on what he had read. A lifetime devoted to this activity slowly made my grandfather into someone who could draw upon his memory at any time to find guidance from God. Although he

. . . A life founded on ungodly counsel ends in futility.

lived through the Great Depression, World War II, and numerous family crises, he felt himself to be blessed. The secret lay in his delight in and meditation on the ways of God.

Consequences (1:3–5)

The psalmist insisted our decisions matter. If we focus on God's ways, we develop a blessed life. Contrariwise, a life founded on ungodly counsel ends in futility.

Verse 3 employs a classic image to describe the blessed life: "a tree planted by streams of water." For many years I found it difficult to appreciate the full import of the image. I grew up in an area of the country blessed with ample rainfall and numerous streams. Trees and other plant life thrived. The psalmist, though, lived in a more arid region. In his world, trees prospered only when planted near natural water supplies or canals.

If we structure our assumptions, perspective, and actions on any basis other than God and God's ways, we build unstable lives.

Such trees grew, produced fruit in season, and resisted disease well.

One young woman applied the verse to her life, saying, "I want to build a life strong enough to hold up in good and bad times, and I want my life to produce results Jesus would be proud to claim. This verse tells me the only way to do so is to root myself in

God. I mean, a tree stakes everything on where it puts down its roots. I have to do the same with God." Talk about preaching an entire sermon in four sentences. She caught the spirit of Psalm 1.

Verses 4–5 spell out the consequences of a life built on ungodly counsel. The psalmist again drew on an image familiar to all in his time. Farmers took the sheaves of grain harvested from their fields and placed them on platforms to dry. The farmers then repeatedly tossed the dry sheaves into the air. Because of its weight and shape, grain fell back to the threshing floor. The lightweight chaff blew away in the wind.

God is alive, active, and watching over those who pursue his way.

If we structure our assumptions, perspective, and actions on any basis other than God and God's ways, we build unstable lives. Such lives cannot stand up under God's scrutiny, now or in eternity.

The Presence of God (1:6)

The psalm starkly calls for us to decide between two ways of life. Frankly, many people might respond by saying the psalmist calls us to undertake an impossible approach to life. In daily life the laws or guidelines of the "wicked," "sinners," and "mockers" (1:1) often seem to get results! The ways of God, by contrast, may involve us in conflict with our culture and take us out of the race for security founded on wealth and position. Why would anyone choose to risk the way endorsed by the psalmist?

Verse 6 provides the answer: God is alive, active, and watching over those who pursue his way. When all is said and done, those who opt to delight in the law of the Lord also choose to rely on God to sustain them. Christians should not be surprised at the psalmist's insistence that they trust God enough to live God's way. After all, Jesus did.

Hebrew Poetry and Parallelism

When we try to interpret the psalms, we must keep in mind they are Hebrew poems. A technique Bible scholars call *parallelism* played a significant role in such poems. The poet used successive lines of poetry to drive home a message. Two or three lines composed a unit of thought. The lines might be *synonymous, antithetical,* or *synthetic.*

Synonymous line sets deal with a common theme. The poet would take a single theme and provide images to reveal various nuances to its meaning. Psalm 1:2 provides an example. The blessed person is one whose "delight is in the law of the Lord." The second line states a similar meaning: "on his law he meditates day and night."

As the term *antithetical* implies, antithetical line sets feature opposing ideas or images. Psalm 1:6 provides a good example. The first line states: "For the Lord watches over the way of the righteous." The second states the opposite: "But the way of the wicked will perish."

Synthetic parallel lines modify a central image or theme by means of simple lists or short phrases. Many scholars consider Psalm 133:1 a prime illustration: "How good and pleasant it is when brothers live together in unity."

In addition, a *combined* or *mixed* type combines two of these patterns. See, for example, Psalm 68:6, in which the first and second lines are synonymous and the third line is antithetical.

What Actions Might We Take?

- Start a personal Bible reading program designed to expose you repeatedly to the Psalms, the Ten Commandments, and the Sermon on the Mount.
- Start a personal journal in which you record your Scripture readings and apply them to building a way of life that brings honor to God.
- Develop a list of the characteristics you would expect to see in someone who took delight in the law of God as Psalm 1 describes such a practice. Share your list with your fellow Sunday School class members as a reminder and inspiration.

Questions

1. Do you know (or did you know) someone whose life seemed to be centered on the ways of God? What did you see in him or her to convince you this was so?

2. What is your personal definition of the happy or blessed life?

3. If you were advising a young Christian how to build a blessed life, what would you say?

4. If you had to make a list of the kinds of unwise counsel available in our time, what would you include?

Focal Text

Psalms 3; 13; 22:1–5, 22–24

Background

Psalms 3; 6; 13; 22

Main Idea

Although God can seem distant and unresponsive to our pleas for help, we can trust God to care and to respond.

Question to Explore

Have you ever wondered in desperation, *Why is God waiting so long to answer?*

LESSON TWO Pleading for God's Help

Study Aim

To compare the psalmist's experiences and mine of wondering why God was waiting so long to respond to my pleas for help

Study and Action Emphases

- Affirm the Bible as our authoritative guide for life and ministry
- Develop a growing, vibrant faith
- Encourage healthy families

Quick Read

When life falls apart, we may wonder whether God knows or cares. Faith becomes an intentional choice in such circumstances. We can trust God to care and respond.

Like many other churches, we housed victims of Hurricane Katrina in 2005. Men, women, boys, and girls arrived to live in our Christian Life Center. Most brought nothing with them but the clothes they wore and various kinds of horrible memories. The storm destroyed their houses, eliminated their jobs, and often separated them from other family members. One woman did not know whether her children had survived. With the help of other churches and nonprofit organizations, we provided shelter, food, clothing, access to medical care, and a host of other basic services. Our volunteers also listened to our guests' stories, prayed for and with them, and generally sought to be the presence of Christ.

We could not take away their pain, fear, shock, and anger. Such natural, human feelings played out at their own pace. Many of our guests were Christians. One elderly man probably spoke for many of them.

"I don't know. I just don't know," he said. "Preacher, I mean it's like this. One minute you're going along and doing all right. The next minute it's all gone. I've gone to church all my life. I've always trusted God. I'm not saying that I've always done the right thing, but I've always trusted God. Well, just now, God seems awfully far away. I just don't know. I wish he would help us."

King David might well have said much the same thing.

Psalm 3

1 O Lord, how many are my foes!
How many rise up against me!
2 Many are saying of me,
"God will not deliver him."
Selah
3 But you are a shield around me, O Lord;
you bestow glory on me and lift up my head.
4 To the Lord I cry aloud,
and he answers me from his holy hill.
Selah
5 I lie down and sleep;
I wake again, because the Lord sustains me.
6 I will not fear the tens of thousands
drawn up against me on every side.
7 Arise, O Lord!
Deliver me, O my God!
Strike all my enemies on the jaw;
break the teeth of the wicked.
8 From the Lord comes deliverance.
May your blessing be on your people.
Selah

Psalm 13

1 How long, O Lord? Will you forget me forever?
How long will you hide your face from me?
2 How long must I wrestle with my thoughts
and every day have sorrow in my heart?
How long will my enemy triumph over me?

3 Look on me and answer, O LORD my God.
Give light to my eyes, or I will sleep in death;
4 my enemy will say, "I have overcome him,"
and my foes will rejoice when I fall.
5 But I trust in your unfailing love;
my heart rejoices in your salvation.
6 I will sing to the LORD,
for he has been good to me.

Psalm 22:1–5, 22–24

1 My God, my God, why have you forsaken me?
Why are you so far from saving me,
so far from the words of my groaning?
2 O my God, I cry out by day, but you do not answer,
by night, and am not silent.
3 Yet you are enthroned as the Holy One;
you are the praise of Israel.
4 In you our fathers put their trust;
they trusted and you delivered them.
5 They cried to you and were saved;
in you they trusted and were not disappointed.

• • • • • • • • • • • • • • • • •

22 I will declare your name to my brothers;
in the congregation I will praise you.

23 You who fear the LORD, praise him!
All you descendants of Jacob, honor him!
Revere him, all you descendants of Israel!
24 For he has not despised or disdained
the suffering of the afflicted one;
he has not hidden his face from him
but has listened to his cry for help.

A King Pleads with God (3:1–8)

Psalm 3 marks the beginning of a series of psalms ascribed to David.[1] According to the superscription attached to the psalm, David composed the piece some time after fleeing from his rebellious son Absalom. Certainly the psalm's language reflects such a desperate situation (see 2 Samuel 13—18, especially 18:33).

David's life collapsed when his son rebelled and overthrew him. He lost his throne and very nearly his life. After decades of rule, he found himself once again hiding with a band of followers. In time, David would gather an army and retake his rightful place, but in the immediate aftermath of the rebellion, his cause did not look promising. The pain of his son's betrayal made it difficult for David to think clearly. In such a time, David relied on a strategy he had used throughout his life. He took his troubles to God.[2]

". . . God seems awfully far away. I just don't know. I wish he would help us."

David acknowledged that he could scarcely fathom the number of his foes (Psalm 3:1). The army of Absalom looked to be overwhelming. Few thought David could survive, let alone win. Many thought God had withdrawn his favor from David (Ps. 3:2). In David's time, most people believed bad luck or catastrophe to be a sign of God's wrath on an individual. It is as if they said: *David must have sinned. That's why God took away his throne. David got what he deserved.* Knowing people thought this way must have added to David's pain. He piled the facts and feelings of his situation together in a carefully crafted psalm and offered it to God.

We know from experience how it feels to swing back and forth between despair and faith.

Something remarkable happened: David rediscovered faith even as he shared his fears with God. Psalm 3:2–3 marks the shift in his focus. In 3:1, David described his dire situation. He now affirmed his faith in God. The images employed by David build on each other until they reach a climax in verse 6.

"But you are a shield around me" (Ps. 3:3). Even though he faced numerous foes and had few supporters, David declared he knew God was his shield. Given the situation, David's words qualified as a faith statement.

"You bestow glory on me" (3:3). David spoke these words as a deposed king, as one shorn of his crown and glory by his son's conspiracy and rebellion. The phrase echoed the language used to describe

God's anointing of a king. In essence, David declared: *God alone has the right to select the king of Israel, and he has chosen me. Although I stand alone in the wilderness, without an army, wealth, or crown, still I am the king by the grace of God.* To an outside observer, David's words probably seemed like the sentiments of someone driven mad by grief. David, though, considered his words to be a statement of faith.

"To the LORD I cry aloud, and he answers me" (3:4). David turned first not to foreign allies or various restoration schemes but to God. He declared that God heard and answered him. David spoke such words long before people began to gather to support him in the effort to retake his throne.

"I lie down and sleep; I wake again" (3:5). As did many of us, you may have learned a simple prayer when you were a child. The prayer began with the words "Now I lay me down to sleep; I pray the Lord my soul to keep." The betrayed king took no credit for his own survival. Instead David declared he lived through his hard days and nights only because God sustained him.

Psalm 13 calls us to bring our strongest feelings to God, even in the most trying times.

"I will not fear" (3:6). David had faced up to the awfulness of his situation (3:1). Yet he had chosen to reaffirm his faith in God (3:2–5). He now felt able to make another decision: to lay aside fear. If we possessed no other psalm from David, we might conclude he moved rather quickly from despair to hope in God.

An Honest Question (13:1–6)

Psalm 13 reveals another aspect of David's reaction to severe adversity. The psalm opens with a heartfelt question: "How long, O LORD?" Many of us have asked the same question during prolonged, difficult periods in our lives.

The psalmist sketched his feelings in a few phrases. A paraphrase of his lament might read as follows: *I feel as if you have forgotten me, God. I'm afraid you will never remember me! Do you know how I feel? My mind is confused. I can't make sense of my situation. My heart is crushed. I feel so sad. My enemies' victories over me grate on my soul!*

When my father wanted to get the attention of my brother or me, he said, "You had better look at me when I'm talking to you." The psalmist, driven by his feelings, took a somewhat similar tack with God. He demanded that God look at him, respond to him, and thereby give him hope. Without such hope the psalmist felt he would die.

God is not intimidated or angered by our feelings or by what we may say to him.

The psalmist's mood shifts abruptly in verse 5. Echoing the conclusion of Psalm 3, he once again chose to trust God. He declared he would place his faith in God's steady love, which he had experienced throughout his life prior to the current crisis.

Psalm 13 rings true, doesn't it? You and I probably can not match its poetry, but we understand the kinds of emotions described. We know from experience how it feels to swing back and forth between despair and faith.

During my late childhood I fell into private but deep despair over my family life. My father's alcoholism negatively affected every aspect of my life. Many nights I lay in bed and wondered why God did not do something to help us. I do not remember everything I might have said to God, but I think Psalm 13:1–5 captures the range of my comments.

A local businessman made a point of stopping by our house each Sunday morning to see whether I wanted to attend church. I usually accepted his invitation. During the worship services, a verse of Scripture, a hymn, a prayer, or some thought that strayed into my mind often shifted my mood. For at least a little while on Sunday morning, I felt God knew where I lived and that he cared. At such times I chose, in ways appropriate to a child, to trust God.

> *Teachers, members of my extended family, local farmers, and business leaders—all taught me by their example that the kind of world I knew in my home was not the only kind of world possible.*

Psalm 13 calls us to bring our strongest feelings to God, even in the most trying times. God is not intimidated or angered by our feelings or by what we may say to him. At the same time, Psalm 13 offers hope. Like David, we may be granted the ability to remember and trust in God's unfailing love, even when we can not sense his presence.

Can Good Be Brought Out of Our Suffering? (22:1–5, 22–24)

Christians usually recognize the opening sentence of Psalm 22. Jesus cited this psalm from the cross (Matthew 27:46; Mark 15:34): "My God, my God, why have you forsaken me?" The psalmist felt utterly abandoned by God, even as he suffered agony at the hands of his persecutors.

To add to his pain, the psalmist could not fathom why God allowed him to suffer. After all, in the past God had acted to save his people (Ps. 22:3–5). Now, though, the psalmist felt worthless (22:6). He felt the ridicule others threw at him (22:7–8). He lost his courage (22:14–15).

The psalmist refused to make despair his last word. In verses 22–24, he declared he would yet praise God's name in the midst of God's people. He exhorted those who knew his sufferings to honor and trust God. The psalmist went further and declared God had not forgotten him in his afflictions but instead had heard his cry for help. In verses 25–31, the psalmist hinted that his suffering might yet serve a purpose in God's greater plans. He dared dream his anguish might play a role in bringing all kinds of people to acknowledge their need for God and worship him. Such proved to be the

" . . . I now see faith might be possible for me in spite of the trouble in my life."

case. The very psalms that convey David's pain and hope have drawn untold numbers of people to God.

Christians believe the suffering of Jesus fulfilled such a role. He opened the way for us to experience God's presence, forgiveness, and love. On a smaller scale, the psalmist's hope can be fulfilled in our lives.

Decades have passed since I was a child dealing with my father's alcoholism. Looking back I now see how God worked to bring some good from the pain of my childhood. Mostly God sent caring adults into my life. Teachers, members of my extended family, local farmers, and business leaders—all taught me by their example that the kind of world I knew in my home was not the only kind of world possible. They planted hope in my heart. Through their caring ministry I came to believe it possible to trust God.

What might the story of your life have to say about suffering and faith?

Eventually I learned to share my story with others. Many times they found something in my tale they needed to hear. As one man said to me, "Hearing you talk about your experiences and feelings and how you have learned to try to trust God, helped me. I now see faith might be possible for me in spite of the trouble in my life."

The psalm reminds us of the power of honest testimony to draw others to God. What might the story of your life have to say about suffering and faith?

David and Absalom

The story of David and his son Absalom is found in 2 Samuel 13:1—19:8. David's family exhibited traits most modern readers would label *dysfunctional.* For example, one of David's sons, Amnon, raped his half-sister Tamar, the full sister of Absalom. David, although furious, chose not to punish Amnon. Two years later, Absalom arranged the murder of Amnon. Absalom went into hiding for three years, after which David allowed him to return to Jerusalem.

Absalom plotted to usurp the throne of David. He made himself popular by commiserating with those who felt David no longer paid attention to the common people. In time Absalom gathered enough support to force David to flee from Jerusalem. Over the course of the following year, the king worked to put together a force that could retake his throne. Finally, the king's general, Joab, led a successful battle against Absalom's forces. Joab killed Absalom. David's grief for his son nearly cost him the loyalty of his own troops. Finally Joab persuaded David to lay aside his grief and reclaim his kingdom.

What Actions Might We Take?

- Identify and pray for those who suffer.
- Think back to a time when you experienced a faith-threatening circumstance; write out a short

testimony of how you came through such a trying time.

- Commit to participate regularly in corporate and personal worship in order to prepare yourself for times that may challenge your faith in God.
- Ask your church's history committee to research and publish stories of times when your church faced adversity and yet emerged with renewed faith and vision.

Questions

1. Read 2 Samuel 13:1—19:8. How would you describe the relationship between David and Absalom? What elements in the relationship might have caused David the greatest grief in the aftermath of the rebellion led by Absalom?

2. What legitimate roles can personal testimonies of suffering and faith play?

3. Did David's lifelong history of worship affect the way he responded to adversity? If so, how?

4. What do you think we should do or say when dealing with people of faith whose lives have been torn apart by catastrophes or the actions of others?

NOTES

1. See the superscriptions to Psalms 3—41; 51—72; 138—145.
2. The psalms in this lesson—Psalms 3; 6; 13; 22—are classified as individual laments. See the small article, "Psalms of Lament," in lesson 4.

Focal Text

Psalms 23; 27:1–6

Background

Psalms 23; 27

Main Idea

We can trust in God's care even when the worst that can happen happens.

Question to Explore

Can we trust God to care for us in the worst of times?

LESSON THREE Trusting in a Caring God

Study Aim

To affirm that we can trust God to care for us even in the worst of times

Study and Action Emphases

- Affirm the Bible as our authoritative guide for life and ministry
- Share the gospel with all people
- Develop a growing, vibrant faith

Quick Read

All of us experience bad times. The psalmist insisted we can trust God to provide for our deepest needs, even when the worst that can happen happens.

Tim stood tall and straight, ate like a teenaged boy, and never missed a chance to participate in a church or community event. When asked the secret of his eighty-plus years, he usually replied: "I try to do the right thing and trust God."

Tim's health finally broke. Following serious brushes with death, Tim was confined to a wheelchair. Various daily medications and a highly restricted diet complicated his life. His voice, once booming, shrank to a whisper.

The last time I saw Tim, I held his hand and asked how he was doing. Tim responded: "I try to do the right thing and trust God." Tim's words echoed the sentiments of the psalmist. He bore testimony to one of our core convictions: We can trust ourselves to God's care even in the worst of circumstances.

Psalm 23

1 The Lord is my shepherd, I shall not be in want.
2 He makes me lie down in green pastures,
he leads me beside quiet waters,
3 he restores my soul.
He guides me in paths of righteousness
for his name's sake.
4 Even though I walk
through the valley of the shadow of death,
I will fear no evil,
for you are with me;

your rod and your staff,
they comfort me.
5 You prepare a table before me
in the presence of my enemies.
You anoint my head with oil;
my cup overflows.
6 Surely goodness and love will follow me
all the days of my life,
and I will dwell in the house of the LORD
forever.

Psalm 27:1–6

1 The LORD is my light and my salvation—
whom shall I fear?
The LORD is the stronghold of my life—
of whom shall I be afraid?
2 When evil men advance against me
to devour my flesh,
when my enemies and my foes attack me,
they will stumble and fall.
3 Though an army besiege me,
my heart will not fear;
though war break out against me,
even then will I be confident.
4 One thing I ask of the LORD,
this is what I seek:
that I may dwell in the house of the LORD
all the days of my life,

to gaze upon the beauty of the LORD
  and to seek him in his temple.
5 For in the day of trouble
  he will keep me safe in his dwelling;
he will hide me in the shelter of his tabernacle
  and set me high upon a rock.
6 Then my head will be exalted
  above the enemies who surround me;
at his tabernacle will I sacrifice with shouts of joy;
  I will sing and make music to the LORD.

The Shepherd Lord (23:1–6)

When I paid a visit to a dying man in the hospital, I found him connected to various pieces of technology. We had never met, but I knew he had little if any connection to Christianity. He was known as a self-made man and a tough business competitor. When I entered the room, he looked straight into my eyes.

"You're that preacher, aren't you?" he asked. I confessed to the charge. He went on: "Got your Bible with you?" I took a pocket edition of the Gospels and Psalms from my coat pocket. "I want you to read something for me," he said. "I don't know where to find it, but it starts out something like 'the Lord is my shepherd.'"

"I try to do the right thing and trust God."

"I think you want to hear the twenty-third psalm," I replied. I read the psalm to him. He settled back in the bed and said, "Yeah, that's the one. Thanks."

The experience reminded me of the pervasive influence of the twenty-third psalm. Most of us can recite the first verse. We may even have memorized the entire psalm at some point in our lives. Even people with little or no relationship to the church often know the twenty-third psalm.

We can trust ourselves to God's care even in the worst of circumstances.

The twenty-third psalm belongs to a group of psalms usually called "hymns of trust." Such psalms celebrate God's dependable and effective care for us. The six verses of the twenty-third psalm provide classic images and phrases to describe what God does.

Shepherds lived with their sheep. They knew and treated each sheep as an individual. At night, a good shepherd lay across the entrance to the sheep pen. He, in effect, sacrificed his body's comfort to protect the sheep from their tendency to stray and from predators who might try to attack them. A shepherd devoted both his days and his nights to the care of the sheep.

"The Lord is my shepherd" (Psalm 23:1). The psalmist used the term *Yahweh*, which we translate as "Lord." In doing so, the psalmist conjured up memories of God's past care of his people. The Lord who shepherded him was the same Lord who had appeared to Moses, led the children of Israel through the wilderness, and dealt with them over the centuries.

What did such a shepherd Lord do? He made the psalmist "lie down in green pastures" (Ps. 23:2). Good grass could not be found everywhere in Palestine. Good shepherds knew where to look. Once they had led their sheep to such pastures, shepherds calmed the sheep so that they would eat and settle down to digest their food. Knowing sheep usually refuse to drink from troubled waters, shepherds led them to "quiet waters" (23:2). The psalmist claimed God always provided the right kinds of provision and rest.

"He restores my soul," wrote the psalmist (23:3). "Soul" translates the Hebrew term *nephesh*. What does it mean? At its fullest, *nephesh* refers to the kind of life God breathes into all of us, the sort of life God intends us to have and enjoy. The psalmist declared God the Shepherd restored him to such a life.

God is the master restorer of the human soul.

Perhaps you have heard someone say—or said yourself, *I feel as if the life is being squeezed out of me.* You and I use such words when tragedy or other circumstances rob us of joy, purpose, and energy. Some friends once saw this happening to me, and so they arranged for me to get away for a few days. Although reluctant to do so, I agreed. I spent several days resting, walking, praying, reading, and allowing my mind to wander. By the time I returned to work, I felt like a new (or renewed) person. Looking back, I believe God guided me through the intervention of my friends. He took me to a place where I could lie down, take nourishment, and experience soul restoration. God is the master restorer of the human soul.

According to the psalmist, God not only restored him but also guided him "in paths of righteousness" (23:3). As daylight ebbed, a shepherd gathered the flock and led them toward home. The way home most often led through the wilderness. Even so, the shepherd led the sheep on a good path, a right path. The term "righteousness" means *to stand upright or straight.* God restores our souls so that we can engage the rough and tumble of daily life in ways that please him.

"I don't know where to find it, but it starts out something like 'the Lord is my shepherd.'"

In order to get home, a shepherd might lead his flock through deep valleys (23:4), where the setting sun's light did not reach. Dangerous beasts and robbers sometimes inhabited such valleys. The shepherd might well have to defend the sheep with his rod. If a sheep stumbled into a crevice, the shepherd used his staff to lift the animal out. Most important of all, the shepherd stayed with the flock. His familiar presence gave the flock the confidence to keep moving through the dark gorge.

We usually associate verse 4 with death, hence our frequent use of Psalm 23 at memorial services. The psalmist had something else in mind. He knew that living a life pleasing to God led to times of danger.

He declared he could endure such times because of God's ongoing presence and care.

The psalmist shifted to a new set of images in verse 5. He depicted God as a gracious host to a desert traveler beset by numerous enemies. The psalmist thought of his life as a dangerous journey. He might well travel through barren places and endure unending attacks from adversaries. How could he hope to endure? The answer lay with God. In the ancient Middle East a good host protected his guests. A strong host might well hold even a horde of enemies at bay, even as he spread a feast for his guest. Since God was his host, the psalmist need not be afraid.

God restores our souls so that we can engage the rough and tumble of daily life in ways that please him.

In verse 6, the psalmist summed up his perspective. He knew now that God never left his side. God knew and provided for all his deepest needs, was able and willing to guide him, and would stand between him and those who might wish to interfere in his journey.

I sometimes kept a journal when I was a teenager. Recently while looking over some of the entries, I found the following comment on Psalm 23: "This means God is always with me. I don't have to try to do this Christian thing on my own. That's good news." The language may not have been elegant, but I think the psalmist might approve.

The Sheltering Lord (27:1–6)

Psalm 27:1–6 also falls into the category "hymns of trust." The psalmist introduced several images, declared he did not have to live in fear of his enemies, and made one petition.

He described God as his "light," "salvation," and "stronghold" (Ps. 27:1). "The Lord is my light," the psalmist said. Darkness confuses the senses and provides cover to potentially dangerous foes. If we are honest, most of us will admit we grow afraid when stranded in the dark. Fear itself is a kind of darkness. Light dispels darkness, enabling us to see clearly and find our way.

The term rendered "salvation" often referred to deliverance. Not only did God light the psalmist's way, but the Lord also rescued him from his foes. The word translated "stronghold" is derived from a word meaning *to strengthen*. The psalmist claimed God as his refuge and the source of his strength.

The psalmist claimed God as his refuge and the source of his strength.

The psalmist announced he did not need to be afraid of those who would hurt him. His courage rested on his confidence in God. The words remind me of the situation faced by King David when his son Absalom rebelled against him (2 Samuel 13—18; see Ps. 3 in lesson 2). David barely escaped the coup with his life. For a year or more, he lived in fear of his enemies, the ones who wished to "devour" him or end his life. David's chances of survival, let alone regaining his throne, looked slim to any objective observer. Still, David refused to give in to numbing despair. He declared he would not fear his enemies but instead would trust God to deal with them.

The psalmist asked but one thing of God: to dwell in God's presence all the days of his life (27:4–6). Whether life brought trouble or joy, the psalmist knew his heart's deepest desire. He wanted to experience the ongoing presence of God. God's presence made the psalmist feel secure. Nothing less would suffice.

Verses 7–12 play an important role in the psalm. The psalmist began to plead with God to listen to him, forgive him, and restore him. Like us, the psalmist's moods alternated between extremes.

Verses 13–14, though, return to the theme of confidence in God. What was the psalmist to do? He must wait for the Lord to take action. In the meantime, he must nurture his faith in God.

Shepherds

Early in the history of Israel, most people relied on flocks for their livelihood. Whatever else might be said of Abraham, Isaac, and Jacob, they were shepherds. One's wealth was measured by the size and quality of one's flocks.

As time passed, the Israelites shifted toward a society based on commerce as well as agriculture. Villages and towns developed, and Jerusalem became an urban center. Most shepherds no longer owned anything. Instead, they were hired hands for absentee owners. People held them in low regard either for social or religious reasons.

David, as the youngest son, drew the unwelcome task of shepherding his father's flock. Ironically, the strength, courage, perseverance, self-sacrificial attitude, and compassion he developed on the job were the very qualities God wanted in Israel's king. Later generations of God's people looked back on David as the ideal king.

David's experience as a shepherd prepared him to comprehend and tell of God's care. Jesus took David's image of God as the Good Shepherd and applied it to himself (John 10:1–18).

Case Study

A prominent, middle-aged Christian businessman in my town developed an aggressive cancer that was not susceptible to treatment. Although shocked by the news, he soon began quietly to put his affairs in order. He made every effort to worship, pray, give, and minister as he had before the onset of cancer.

I asked him to speak at one of our morning worship services. He gave a simple testimony of how he trusted Christ to walk with him through the experience. At the end of his presentation, he gently urged us to choose to give life as well as death into God's hands. A young adult told me, "That's the most powerful testimony I've every heard. You can't help but take such a man seriously."

What elements in the man's life or testimony contributed to his credibility?

Questions

1. What Scriptures would you want read to you if you were in great distress or dying? Why?

2. If you were asked to replace the images of the shepherd and host in Psalm 23 with images drawn from contemporary life, which ones would you select? Why?

3. Psalm 27 reveals both the psalmist's faith and his doubt. Do you experience mood swings in terms of your own faith? Do you know someone who does? If so, what do you think accounts for such shifts?

4. Do you share the assurance the psalmist felt when he wrote, "I will dwell in the house of the LORD forever" (23:6)? What difference does this sense of assurance make to your daily decision-making?

Focal Text

Psalms 42—43

Background

Psalms 42—43

Main Idea

A sense of God's presence is so essential to life that a sense of God's absence and distance is troubling.

Question to Explore

Do most people today long for God's presence?

LESSON FOUR

Thirsting for God

Study Aim

To describe the psalmist's experience of thirsting for God and identify ways for helping someone (perhaps yourself) who feels distant from God

Study and Action Emphases

- Affirm the Bible as our authoritative guide for life and ministry
- Develop a growing, vibrant faith

Quick Read

People of faith find it painful when they cannot sense God's presence. Psalms 42—43 treat such circumstances as occasions for worship and encourage us to continue to place our hope in God.

A long-term Christian once sat across the desk from me and said, "I don't know if I can stand much more. It's as if God packed his bags and left town. I don't know if he is coming back. I miss him so much, and I'm afraid without him. What's wrong with me? Is this normal?"

We talked for some time. Finally, I suggested we read Psalms 42 and 43 aloud. We did so. When we finished, my friend said, "That's me. That's how I feel. I want to believe I'll sense God in my life again. I also want to tell God how bad it feels when I can't sense his presence. What do you think?"

"I think," I replied, "that Psalms 42 and 43 grant us permission to feel strongly both ways at the same time. They give scriptural warrant to our fears and our one great hope. To my way of thinking, God speaks through the two psalms, letting us know such mixed feelings are normal, even for people of faith. Did you know the psalms were used in public worship in ancient Israel? Through the psalms, the people of God offered God such feelings as an act of worship. They seem to have believed such an offering pleased God and helped them as well."

Augustine of Hippo (A.D. 354–430) wrote, "Thou hast made us for thyself and restless is our heart until it comes to rest in thee."[1] Christians through the centuries have found this to be case. The psalmist helps us deal with our longing for God. In Psalms 42—43, he described how it feels not to be able to sense God's presence, and he modeled how to anchor ourselves in such times.

Psalm 42

1 As the deer pants for streams of water,
so my soul pants for you, O God.
2 My soul thirsts for God, for the living God.
When can I go and meet with God?
3 My tears have been my food
day and night,
while men say to me all day long,
"Where is your God?"
4 These things I remember
as I pour out my soul:
how I used to go with the multitude,
leading the procession to the house of God,
with shouts of joy and thanksgiving
among the festive throng.
5 Why are you downcast, O my soul?
Why so disturbed within me?
Put your hope in God,
for I will yet praise him,
my Savior and 6 my God.
My soul is downcast within me;
therefore I will remember you
from the land of the Jordan,
the heights of Hermon—from Mount Mizar.

7 Deep calls to deep
in the roar of your waterfalls;
all your waves and breakers
have swept over me.
8 By day the Lord directs his love,
at night his song is with me—
a prayer to the God of my life.
9 I say to God my Rock,
"Why have you forgotten me?
Why must I go about mourning,
oppressed by the enemy?"
10 My bones suffer mortal agony
as my foes taunt me,
saying to me all day long,
"Where is your God?"
11 Why are you downcast, O my soul?
Why so disturbed within me?
Put your hope in God,
for I will yet praise him,
my Savior and my God.

Psalm 43

1 Vindicate me, O God,
and plead my cause against an ungodly nation;
rescue me from deceitful and wicked men.
2 You are God my stronghold.
Why have you rejected me?
Why must I go about mourning,
oppressed by the enemy?

3 Send forth your light and your truth,
  let them guide me;
let them bring me to your holy mountain,
  to the place where you dwell.
4 Then will I go to the altar of God,
  to God, my joy and my delight.
I will praise you with the harp,
  O God, my God.
5 Why are you downcast, O my soul?
  Why so disturbed within me?
Put your hope in God,
  for I will yet praise him,
  my Savior and my God.

First Lament (42:1–4)

Psalms 42 and 43 comprise a single unit of thought and are best read together. The psalmist presented three personal laments and three identical refrains. A student once asked me to give her a shorthand description of the poem's movements. I responded: "The psalmist tells God how bad things are three times. After each lament, he then tells himself to trust God anyway."

The psalmist began by comparing his longing for God to a great thirst. Like a deer desperate for water in a parched land, the psalmist yearned for a sense of God's presence. Such an animal grew more frantic as it found familiar water holes dry. The psalmist felt much the same way. He yearned for "the living God" (Psalm 42:2), the God best experienced in the present moment.

When can I go and meet with God? The psalmist's words may be interpreted in one of two ways. One school of thought suggests he had been cut off from the temple by enemies, disease, or other causes. Exiled from the place in which he had worshiped, he felt bereft of God's presence and wondered when he might be allowed to return to the temple. Others think the psalmist lamented a change in his heart, which rendered him incapable of sensing God's presence as in the past. In either case, the psalmist grieved his loss.

> *"It's as if God packed his bags and left town."*

Others added to the psalmist's pain by mocking him and his God. They knew the psalmist's former condition, how he once displayed public confidence in the presence and power of God. Perhaps in earlier times he had tried to persuade them to trust his God. Now they saw his despair and helplessness, and they also saw he could not sense God. At best, some may have tried to persuade him to give up on God. The majority probably ridiculed him.

Memory fed his pain. The psalmist recalled how he used to enjoy joining with other worshipers in worship at the temple. He remembered being caught up in the experience. Some commentators speculate the psalmist was of the priestly group and that he once had led worship processions. Whether he had been a priest or a common worshiper, the psalmist's memories of such good days added to his present sense of loss.

The Refrain of Hope (42:5)

Suddenly the psalmist burst into a refrain of hope. Have you ever lectured yourself? The psalmist asked himself a telling question: "Why are you downcast, O my soul? Why so disturbed within me?" It is as if he said to himself, *Yes, I know I have genuine reasons for despair. I've just finished cataloging a few. Still, given what I remember about the presence and power of God, why should I settle for despondency?* He chose to put his hope in the God he currently could not sense, declaring that he would yet praise God.

> *"The psalmist tells God how bad things are three times. After each lament, he then tells himself to trust God anyway."*

The psalmist's refrain of hope implies that the decision to stake one's life on God is a matter of will rather than feelings. The reality of a caring God does not depend on our ability to sense God's presence. Sometimes you or I are in such a mood that although we stand in the bright light of the sun, we feel as if the sky is covered by dark clouds. Our feelings do not change reality, though. The sun still shines. The psalmist knew this to be so. Therefore, even in the midst of his worst moments, he dared hope for a better future.

Second Lament (42:6–10)

Emotions matter, though. No sooner had the psalmist declared his decision to place his hope in God than his heart dragged him once again into the depths of despair. Although he chose to believe he might again experience the presence of God at some point in time, still he could not deny his present pain.

He chose to put his hope in the God he currently could not sense, declaring that he would yet praise God.

Verses 6–7 feature images that may confuse us. We are in good company, for scholars divide over their interpretation as well. I think the psalmist retreated once again to the resource of his memory. He felt exiled from the temple, the place where he had so often encountered the living God. In verse 6, he confessed he no longer could sense God anywhere in Israel. Even the sound of the waterfalls in the mountains reminded him only of how he felt overwhelmed by waves of sorrow. Every sight and sound served only to remind him of his loss.

We understand his feelings, don't we? An aunt of mine lost an adult daughter to death. The young woman and her mother had been very close. I was only a small boy at the time, but I remember my aunt telling us how she could not bear to go into her daughter's room. All the books and keepsakes that testified to the joys they had shared now broke her heart. The psalmist's grief worked in similar fashion.

The psalmist tried to manipulate God (42:8–9). He reminded God of God's responsibilities as his God. In effect, the psalmist said: *God, you need to start acting like God. It's your job to make certain I'm aware of your love and presence. If you're the foundation (the rock) of my life, you must make certain I can feel you beneath my feet. With all due respect, God, you're not getting the job done. If you were, I would not feel as if my bones were melting away, and I would not be at the mercy of my derisive enemies.* The psalmist attempted to shame God into making his presence felt.

> *The reality of a caring God does not depend on our ability to sense God's presence.*

The Refrain of the Hope Repeated (42:11)

When my daughter was very small and did not get her way, she sometimes fell into a rage. With all the energy a tiny child could muster, she would inform me in no uncertain terms that if I really loved her I would do what she wanted. Eventually, she vented her emotions, settled down, and decided I might love her even if I did not fulfill her wishes.

Something similar happened to the psalmist. Having momentarily exhausted his anger against

God, he returned to his senses. Once again he sang his refrain of hope. In spite of how he felt about his situation, regardless of his disappointment with God, still he chose to place his hope in God.

Third Lament (43:1–4)

After catching his breath, the psalmist offered a third lament. He pleaded with God to vindicate him and to defend him against all his foes. His words revealed his sense of isolation not only from God but from his fellow Israelites, whom he characterized as ungodly (43:1).

. . . Even in the midst of his worst moments, he dared hope for a better future.

The psalmist confessed he had no one to turn to other than God, his "stronghold" or strength (43:2). Once again he wondered whether he had done something to offend God, for surely there had to be some reason for his suffering.

He made a promise to God. The psalmist asked God to send out guides, who would lead the psalmist back into God's presence. His imagination remained limited in that he could not conceive they might take him anywhere other than the temple, which rested on God's holy mount and which contained the altar of God. If only God would lead him there, the psalmist promised he would offer God joyful, music-filled worship.

The Refrain of Hope Repeated (43:5)

For the last time the psalmist repeated his refrain of hope (see 42:5, 11). Although he had yet to sense any response from God, still he chose to cast his lot with God. Perhaps God would act in due time in a way he could not yet imagine. In any case, he told himself, "Put your hope in God, for I will yet praise him, my Savior and my God."

Psalms of Lament

Laments come in two types, laments of the community and personal laments. The term *lament* may be misleading. We often understand the term to imply only sadness, despair, or pessimism. The psalmists certainly dealt with such themes, but they fashioned psalms in order to place their pain before God. In effect, they gave suffering a proper place within the larger context of the worship of God.

Most laments contained the following elements: salutation or address to God, complaint(s), confession(s) of trust, petition(s), some assurance that God will hear the psalmist's words, and a concluding promise to trust or call on God.

Psalms of lament put raw, human emotion on display. The psalmists cried out for protection from their enemies and deliverance from whatever oppressed them. They described the full range of human suffering. If the psalmist was angry or disappointed with God, he said so. At the same time, the psalms of lament feature a determination to continue to call on God. Because of the way such psalms fuse the human condition with the conviction of God's reality and love, they often have sparked worship renewal throughout church history.

What Actions Might We Take?

- Make a commitment to share your deepest feelings with God.
- Ask God to help you be the presence of Christ in the life of someone who is lonely or who is suffering in some other way.
- Begin to pray at least once a day that God might make you aware of his presence.
- Begin to pray at least once a day that God might make his presence felt in your church family.

Questions

1. What worship settings or experiences in your past gave you a strong sense of God's presence?

2. What recent worship settings or experiences have given you a strong sense of God's presence?

3. If the author of Psalms 42—43 asked you to tell him what you thought of these psalms, what might you say?

4. If you have experienced periods during which you found it difficult or impossible to sense the presence of God, what resources helped you through the ordeal?

NOTES

1. Augustine, *Confessions*, I.1.

Focal Text

Psalm 73

Background

Psalm 73

Main Idea

When we doubt the worth of believing in God, we need to get a fresh perspective on what life is all about.

Question to Explore

Is being faithful to God really worthwhile?

LESSON FIVE

Almost Doubting

Study Aim

To describe the psalmist's experience of almost doubting and to state reasons for being faithful to God

Study and Action Emphases

- Affirm the Bible as our authoritative guide for life and ministry
- Share the gospel with all people
- Develop a growing, vibrant faith

Quick Read

Sometimes our life experiences create challenges to our faith. When that happens, we should confidently take our concerns to God. We can trust God to grant us help and understanding.

As my wife and I raised our four children, we had the responsibility of attempting to provide guidance for a number of science projects through the years. I use the word *guidance* liberally, for neither of us is scientifically gifted. When our son Philip was in elementary school, he mixed chemicals to "manufacture" a gas that inflated a balloon stretched over a bottle. At best it was a hit and miss deal, working sporadically. On the day when he demonstrated it for the teachers, what do you know? It worked perfectly. When it did, he looked up at the teachers with a look that said, *Did you see that? It did what it was supposed to do.* Experience validated theory.

We are delighted when what we believe should happen actually occurs, when our experience confirms our convictions. On the other hand, we are disappointed when what we experience in our lives seems to contradict what we profess to believe about God. We hear truths about the love of God on Sunday. We accept them, but then the cruelty or unfairness of life causes us to ask questions. What should we do when we face that kind of confusing circumstance? The author of Psalm 73 faced such an issue. Let's trace his pilgrimage and see if he can help us.

Even as the Israelites credited Moses with giving them five books of law, they credited David with giving them five books of poems that allowed them to express their response to God. Psalm 73 is the first poem in Book III (Psalms 73—89). This third section differs from the first two books in that David is mentioned in the superscriptions in only one psalm (86). The superscriptions include David in all but five (1; 2; 9; 10; 33) of the forty-one poems in Book I (1—41) and in more than half of those in Book II (42—72; see superscriptions of 51—65, 68—70).

The title of Psalm 73 identifies it as "A psalm of Asaph." Asaph was one of the worship leaders or musicians from the tribe of Levi who served the court of King David (1 Chronicles 6:31–32, 39; 16:5; 2 Chronicles 5:12). Asaph's descendants continued to serve in this role before and after the Babylonian exile (2 Chron. 29:13; 35:15; Ezra 3:10; Nehemiah 12:35). Psalm 73 is one of the eleven poems in this "Asaphite hymnal" (Psalms 73—83) or collection that dominates Book III (73—89). Psalm 50 is the only other poem in this collection of Asaph.

Old Testament interpreters have usually classified this psalm as a wisdom poem. Wisdom poems either instructed hearers in the wise way to live (Ps. 1) or wrestled with the confusing mysteries of life (Ps. 37; 49; 73).

This psalmist's "faith world" declared that God would provide many blessings for any who were faithful to him. However, that is not the way the psalmist saw it playing out in the "real world." While the Book of Job dealt with the suffering of a righteous person, this psalm examines the other side of that coin, the prosperity and success of the unrighteous or the wicked.

Psalm 73

1 Surely God is good to Israel,
to those who are pure in heart.
2 But as for me, my feet had almost slipped;
I had nearly lost my foothold.
3 For I envied the arrogant
when I saw the prosperity of the wicked.
4 They have no struggles;
their bodies are healthy and strong.
5 They are free from the burdens common to man;
they are not plagued by human ills.
6 Therefore pride is their necklace;
they clothe themselves with violence.
7 From their callous hearts comes iniquity;
the evil conceits of their minds know no limits.
8 They scoff, and speak with malice;
in their arrogance they threaten oppression.
9 Their mouths lay claim to heaven,
and their tongues take possession of the earth.
10 Therefore their people turn to them
and drink up waters in abundance.
11 They say, "How can God know?
Does the Most High have knowledge?"
12 This is what the wicked are like—
always carefree, they increase in wealth.
13 Surely in vain have I kept my heart pure;
in vain have I washed my hands in innocence.
14 All day long I have been plagued;
I have been punished every morning.

15 If I had said, "I will speak thus,"
I would have betrayed your children.
16 When I tried to understand all this,
it was oppressive to me
17 till I entered the sanctuary of God;
then I understood their final destiny.
18 Surely you place them on slippery ground;
you cast them down to ruin.
19 How suddenly are they destroyed,
completely swept away by terrors!
20 As a dream when one awakes,
so when you arise, O Lord,
you will despise them as fantasies.
21 When my heart was grieved
and my spirit embittered,
22 I was senseless and ignorant;
I was a brute beast before you.
23 Yet I am always with you;
you hold me by my right hand.
24 You guide me with your counsel,
and afterward you will take me into glory.
25 Whom have I in heaven but you?
And earth has nothing I desire besides you.
26 My flesh and my heart may fail,
but God is the strength of my heart
and my portion forever.
27 Those who are far from you will perish;
you destroy all who are unfaithful to you.
28 But as for me, it is good to be near God.
I have made the Sovereign Lord my refuge;
I will tell of all your deeds.

Faith Senses a Contradiction (73:1–12)

The author provided a grammatical key to the structure of his thoughts. "Surely" (73:1, 13, 18) begins each of the three sections. This Hebrew particle contains the note of certainty. It signifies something that is or should be widely accepted.

The psalmist expressed a widely accepted conviction of Israel's faith (73:1). He declared that God showered goodness on those who belonged to him. God would provide and protect anyone who would be faithful to him. "Pure in heart" (73:1) denotes one who approached God with no divided loyalty but a single devotion to God. To the Hebrew people the "heart" was the center of thought and action. The frequency of the word in the psalm marks the theme of this poem as being central to life (73:1, 7, 13, 21, 26).

. . . We are disappointed when what we experience in our lives seems to contradict what we profess to believe about God.

Verse 1 expresses what the psalmist believed, but would that affirmation stand the test of rugged life experience? Biblical faith is not shallow in nature. It is able to withstand any and all challengers and is in fact stronger when it is tested.

The fact of God's goodness to his people was foundational truth; however, the psalmist was in danger of losing confidence in its validity (73:2). He was in danger of losing that foothold because of the evidence he saw everywhere. He was jealous of wicked people who experienced more of the goodness of God than he did. "Prosperity" (73:3) translates the Hebrew word *shalom*. It described the sense of peace and well-being or total contentment people felt when they had everything they needed.

The psalmist catalogued the details of this *shalom*—"prosperity"—of the wicked in verses 4–12. These verses represent a broad generalization on the part of the psalmist, but they are his testimony of what he perceived. The wicked enjoyed a problem-free existence and were not subject to the expected human struggles. "Healthy" (73:4) means *sleek* or *fat*. The Hebrews' concept of a body that appeared to be healthy is the opposite of our emphasis on having a quite thin "runway model" physique. They celebrated robust bodies as the desired picture of happiness and health. The psalmist was saying that God never bothered to punish the wicked, who lived well. "Plagued" (73:5) often carried the connotation of divine discipline.

> *Biblical faith . . . is able to withstand any and all challengers and is in fact stronger when it is tested.*

The wicked arrogantly acted as if they deserved their carefree lives. The psalmist considered them to be proud and loud in their speech and actions (73:6–9). Since people wore gaudy jewelry as a status symbol, wearing pride as a "necklace" (73:6) suggests that they recognized and flaunted their superiority over others.

Verse 9 is a clear example of parallelism, the most important feature of Hebrew poetry (see article, "Hebrew Poetry and Parallelism," in lesson one). In consecutive lines Hebrew poets expressed the same truth either in a similar, progressive, or opposite way. Understanding this characteristic is important to proper interpretation of the poetry in the Old Testament. Notice in verse 9 the "twin statements" or parallelism with regard to their proud boasts: "mouths"/"tongues"; "lay claim"/"take possession"; and "heaven"/"earth."

The fact of God's goodness to his people was foundational truth; however, the psalmist was in danger of losing confidence in its validity (73:2).

The wicked, moreover, have no realization of their evil behavior. They have no room for God in their lives (73:11). Tragically, their arrogant conceit has an influence on others. Probably the meaning of verse 10 is that others are impressed by the good life of the wicked and are drawn to them. The wicked had no problems in the past, and they keep getting richer and richer in the present (73:12). The "lifestyle of the (wicked) rich and famous" seemed to contradict what the psalmist truly believed. The psalmist believed that those who lived pure lives would experience *shalom*—God's blessing. The evidence, though, revealed that wicked people experienced it.

Faith Seeks Comprehension (73:13–17)

The psalmist previously expressed certainty in the faith claim that God was good to his own people and thus that one's faithfulness to God made a difference (73:1). At this point he seems to have been equally convinced that faithfulness to God doesn't really matter at all. He based that thought on the clear contrast that he felt existed between wicked people and him. While they proudly and arrogantly had no regard for God, he had maintained a purity of heart. While they received no discipline or punishment from God, he experienced punishment from God constantly (73:14). "Plagued" in verses 5 and 14 translates the same word. The psalmist concluded that one gains no good or benefit from maintaining a faithfulness to God.

> *The goodness of God is not about what God might give to us. It is God himself.*

Although the psalmist had come to a daring conclusion, he did not dare to express it aloud (73:15). What prevented him from asserting his conclusion publicly was his place in the community of faith. He was unwilling to give up on his faith in God because of his loyalty to the people of God. That is a beautiful reminder of the importance of the powerful bond that unites God's people in mutual accountability. Rich is the person who has an intimate fellow member or dear friend who will be a faithful "accountability partner."

The psalmist could not bring himself to declare what seemed to him to be true. His reluctance may have stemmed from the fact that he had not resolved it in his own mind. In fact, the more he tried to understand the complexity of these issues, the more confused he became. "Oppressive" (73:16) was the dark side of labor for the Hebrew people. It was the word that they used to describe the misery of non-productive or meaningless toil or work.

We have all "been there, done that" in the mode of this psalmist.

Where can one go when one can find no resolution to difficult spiritual issues? The psalmist "entered the sanctuary of God" (73:17). The consensus is that the psalmist enjoyed a memorable worship encounter with God (similar to the one related in Isaiah 6). Since the word "sanctuary" is plural in the Hebrew text, he may have encountered God meaningfully on several occasions. The psalmist came away from the experience(s) of the presence of God changed. This verse is the significant transitional point for the entire psalm. It was the *aha* moment for this follower of God. Note that the turning point did not result from a change in outward circumstances. (The wicked were still arrogant.) Rather, the turning point resulted from a reorientation of the psalmist's understanding. God granted him the vision of the "bigger picture." His testimony to us is that apart from God no resolution exists for this issue.

Faith Speaks a Confirmation (73:18–28)

The psalmist expressed certainty about one last thing. He was now assured specifically that God would bring the wicked (who had everything going for them) to an inglorious end (73:18–20). While the psalmist *almost* slipped (73:2), the wicked will *actually* slip into ruin (73:18).The fantasy of their carefree existence would end up being a nightmare for them. Their destruction would be sudden and complete.

Verses 18–28 show that God successfully resolved the challenge to the psalmist's faith assertion of verse 1. The psalmist was quite ashamed and confessed to God his foolishness in doubting God's goodness (73:21–22). Although we might excuse the psalmist for being merely human, he declared that he had been sub-human or animal-like in his folly.

The final verses reveal how the psalmist came to his life-changing resolution (73:23–28). The answer was the presence of God. In his worship encounters with God, the psalmist remembered that God was always with him (73:23, 25). Previously he thought that good behavior must be rewarded with physical blessings or material benefits. He now knew that the goodness of God to Israel was really seen in their privilege to experience the nearness of God (73:28).

The goodness of God is not about what God might give to us. It is God himself.

This resolution was not merely intellectual or theoretical. The psalmist did not now know everything about why life unfolds as it does for the faithful and the wicked. God has reserved to himself part of that mystery; therefore, the psalmist continually needed the guidance of God (73:24). It appears in this verse that the psalmist has really pushed the boundaries of the conventional Old Testament thinking about life beyond the grave. The Old Testament view was that every person, whether good or bad, went to the same place at death, a place called *Sheol*. The Israelites never used the word underlying "glory" for the abode of the dead (although we sometimes use the word in that sense).

We have wondered . . . why people who have no time or room for God in their lives seem to waltz through life with little or no difficulty to face.

Doubts might arise at some future time for this poet, but he was now secure in his God. When challenges to faith came, he declared that God was the *rock* (literal Hebrew meaning of word translated "strength") of his heart and his "portion" (73:26). The Old Testament uses that latter term to describe the part or share in the land of promise that each Israelite received. Remember that the tribe of Levi did not receive a portion of the land. Each member of the priestly tribe of Levi (as Asaph was) received God as his "portion" (see Deuteronomy 10:9). The psalmist determined to tell others of what he had discovered about God and the mystery of life (73:28).

It is time to admit it. We have all "been there, done that" in the mode of this psalmist. We have wondered (if not overtly complained) why people who have no time or room for God in their lives seem to waltz through life with little or no difficulty to face. We raise questions about fairness and justice. We subject our faith claims to rigorous testing.

God invaded the space of this psalmist in a similar way as he did for Job. He provided neither of them with complete answers about why things happen as they do. He reassured both of them that he would always be with them, and that was enough. It should be enough for us as well.

Sheol

Christians believe that those who trust in Jesus will go to heaven when they die, a place where they will enjoy peace in the presence of God. Non-believers will go to a place of punishment and suffering. In the Old Testament, God's people had no such understanding of life after death. They held that at death all people went to the same place, *Sheol* (Job 30:23).

Sheol was a place of neither perfect bliss nor terrible punishment. *Sheol* was a shadowy existence where people were not fully awake or asleep, a place where there was no memory, praise, thought, or work. It was a place of helplessness and weakness. It was not altogether a grim place, for God was present even in *Sheol* (Ps. 139:8). *Sheol* was not a place, though, where the faithful were rewarded by God or the wicked were punished.

Case Study

They are neighbors but have nothing in common. One family has no time or room for God. The parents have good jobs. The kids are smart. All are in perfect health, and they enjoy their materialistic toys. The other family is a strong Christian one. The mother has a crippling disease. The father faces a downsizing move at work. Their house is the only one on the block that has mold. This couple declares to you that they don't see the point of going to church anymore. They are tired of praying without seeing results. What is your response?

Questions

1. Do you believe that it is a sin for Christians to have doubts about God? Why or why not?

2. Have you ever "envied the arrogant" (73:2)? If you have, what served as the catalyst for your emotion?

3. Have you ever experienced a time of dramatic worship that had such an important impact on you as this psalmist experienced? What caused it to be so pivotal for you?

4. Are you eager or reluctant to share your spiritual pilgrimage with others? What is the potential value of sharing our stories?

LESSON SIX

The Joy of Worshiping God Together

Focal Text

Psalm 84

Background

Psalms 76; 84; 87

Main Idea

Genuinely worshiping God together is an experience of joy.

Question to Explore

Is worshiping God with fellow believers a joy or a chore?

Study Aim

To evaluate my experience of worshiping God with fellow worshipers in light of the psalmist's experience and identify ways for enhancing the experience of corporate worship

Study and Action Emphases

- Affirm the Bible as our authoritative guide for life and ministry
- Develop a growing, vibrant faith

Quick Read

We have the privilege to enjoy the worship of God. It is a gift of grace. Whether we experience that joy may depend on how we prepare for worship.

Recently I had the privilege of spending the Sunday morning Bible study hour with our university students in a question-and-answer time. They composed questions about God and faith and invited me to explore answers with them. We discussed doctrinal issues such as the Trinity and biblical authority as well as some behavioral issues. They also asked me questions about differences in worship styles.

I assured them that modern believers are not the first generation of Christ's followers to experience diversity in the way we offer praise to God. I asserted that for centuries of Christian history some congregations sang only the poems that we find in the Book of Psalms. The church did not accept what we call "traditional hymns" for quite some time after they made an appearance. The Book of Psalms itself is evidence that we can worship God in a diversity of form or style. It contains many different kinds of poems that the Israelites used in their worship.

I encouraged our university students to have some appreciation for those who prefer traditional hymns to contemporary hymns. I have also encouraged our older believers to have appreciation for the contemporary expressions of praise meaningful to younger believers (among others). Worship of God is the one thing that the entire church does together. It is disturbing to me that the one thing that we do together tends to divide us rather than unify us. I wish we could joyfully worship our God together, while recognizing that we have different preferences in worship styles.

Psalm 84 is a hymn of praise to God, but it is a distinctive kind of hymn, one that is called a hymn or song of Zion. Psalms 46, 48, 76, 87, and 122 are also songs of Zion. These poems contain a common theme. They celebrate the reign or rule of God. They especially emphasize God's sovereignty expressed through his king in Jerusalem or Zion. They focus on the might and majesty of the God who conquers all enemies. They are bold and militaristic in nature like Martin Luther's great hymn "A Mighty Fortress Is Our God." While some of the other songs of Zion (like Psalm 76) focus on the conquering power of God's might, Psalm 84 expresses God's tender nature that is available to us in worship times.

The title includes several components. This psalm is one of fifty-five that have the phrase "for the director of music" in the superscription. The root meaning of the Hebrew word is *shine*, but that sheds no light on the specific sense of the term. The word probably communicated some musical instructions. We possess no certainty either for the meaning of the musical term "gittith" (also Ps. 8; 81). The "Sons of Korah" were a group of Levitical priests or musicians similar to the sons of Asaph. We find two collections associated with the sons of Korah (Ps. 42—43, 44—49, 84—85, 87—88).

I have provided my comments on this psalm in an inverted way (by studying the last verses first). Let me explain why. This allows us first to examine the potential benefits of worshiping God joyfully (84:5–12). Knowing the benefits should inspire us then to do the things that are required from us in order to make those benefits possible (84:1–4).

Psalm 84

1 How lovely is your dwelling place,
O LORD Almighty!
2 My soul yearns, even faints,
for the courts of the LORD;
my heart and my flesh cry out
for the living God.
3 Even the sparrow has found a home,
and the swallow a nest for herself,
where she may have her young—
a place near your altar,
O LORD Almighty, my King and my God.
4 Blessed are those who dwell in your house;
they are ever praising you.

Selah

5 Blessed are those whose strength is in you,
who have set their hearts on pilgrimage.
6 As they pass through the Valley of Baca,
they make it a place of springs;
the autumn rains also cover it with pools.
7 They go from strength to strength,
till each appears before God in Zion.
8 Hear my prayer, O LORD God Almighty;
listen to me, O God of Jacob.

Selah

9 Look upon our shield, O God;
look with favor on your anointed one.
10 Better is one day in your courts
than a thousand elsewhere;
I would rather be a doorkeeper in the house of my God
than dwell in the tents of the wicked.
11 For the LORD God is a sun and shield;
the LORD bestows favor and honor;
no good thing does he withhold
from those whose walk is blameless.
12 O LORD Almighty,
blessed is the man who trusts in you.

What We Should Take from Worship (84:5–12)

Worship brings honor to God. It begins with God, and it should end with God. At the same time, the worshiper receives spiritual benefit from being in the presence of God with others. This psalmist designated what some of those benefits are.

First, when we encounter God in worship, we are "blessed" (84:5). This psalm that focuses on worship contains this word "blessed" three times (84:4, 5, 12). These beatitudes remind us that worshiping God, truly experiencing God's presence, grants us the privilege of feeling blessed or being happy and contented.

Second, worshiping God encourages or strengthens us (84:5–7). The Bible elsewhere asserts that this word translated "strength" is a characteristic of the nature of God (Exodus 15:13; Ps. 29:1; 68:35).

God may grant his strength to us directly as we focus our attention on who he is and what he has done for us. On the other hand, God may share his strength with us through the encouragement of fellow worshipers. The psalmist recognized that worshipers traveled to Jerusalem in pilgrimage groups. Sometimes the trip was not an easy one, and they assisted one another when necessary. Interpreters have understood "Valley of Baca" (84:6) to be either a village in Galilee (as the first-century Jewish historian Josephus indicates), a valley of balsam trees (2 Samuel 5:23–24), or a symbolic reference—*valley of tears*—signifying the strains and dangers of travel. The psalmist seems to suggest that in spite of dangers or difficulties, God provides blessing and encouragement.

This principle may be the best rationale for corporate worship. We need to worship God with others because of the reciprocal or mutual strength or encouragement that we receive. We do travel through this life together and need one another to rejoice in the various testimonies of God's grace. We encourage one another through the gift of our very presence. We encourage one another through the sharing of musical and literary gifts. We encourage one another through the spoken testimony of how we have encountered the grace and strength of God.

We have the privilege to pray for one another.

We not only encourage and strengthen one another when we gather for worship. We have the privilege to pray for one another. This is a third benefit of worship. Verse 8 is another clear example of that paramount Hebrew poetry technique—parallelism (see "Hebrew Poetry and Parallelism," lesson one). In this instance, the psalmist says the same thing in two successive lines in a similar way. He requested God to hear (and grant) his petition. Now look in verse 9 at what or whom he prayed for. He prayed for his spiritual and political leader, his king. He mentioned the king with regard to two roles the king filled (Ps. 84:9). To the people he was their "shield" or the one who protected them. Protection of his subjects was one of the principal tasks of ancient kings. To God he was "the anointed one" or the one God had chosen and set apart to lead them. The chosen king would be anointed with olive oil as a symbol of his selection. This word (Hebrew, *messiah*) would not become a technical term for the one God promised to send until after the close of the Old Testament period. Here it simply designated the human king.

> *. . . The desire to serve God is yet another benefit of worship.*

Maybe you have seen a sign that said, "Enter to worship. Depart to serve." Worship and service are certainly inseparable realities. The psalmist accepted that assertion. He had so powerfully encountered the presence of God in just one day of worship that he desired to serve God as an usher, greeter, or "doorkeeper"

(84:10). In fact he would rather be serving God in what some may have considered a menial way than by enjoying leisure in another place. Thus the desire to serve God is yet another benefit of worship. "Tents of the wicked" would signify any place devoted to self-serving tendencies.

The final benefit that one receives from worship is the protection and favor of God (84:11–12).

The final benefit that one receives from worship is the protection and favor of God (84:11–12). We sense God's love and care for us when we worship him. Verse 11 is the only verse in the Old Testament where "sun" is used as a reference to God. Some commentators suggest that the reading should mean *battlement* as a synonym for "shield." The latter part of verse 11 suggests that our God is not stingy, for he willingly shares himself (and the accompanying benefits) with any who will seek to meet him in worship.

What We Should Bring to Worship (84:1–4)

"You will only get something out of it if you put something into it." Many parents have shared that wisdom with their children. It is so true when applied to worship. If we expect to receive the blessings of worship enumerated in Psalm 84:5–12, we must be willing to make the necessary preparation described in the first four verses.

The author of this psalm expressed the same kind of passion as the author of Psalms 42—43 (see lesson four). In those poems, the author was strong in his sadness at being far from the place of worship. In this psalm, though, the poet emphatically rejoiced in the opportunity to gather with others and worship his God.

My wife and I have been privileged to lead several groups to visit the land of the Bible. On our trip to Israel in 2001 we were approaching Jerusalem from Tel Aviv through the foothills (climbing from the coastal area). The guide on our bus was playing a musical tape for us. He timed it perfectly. We were listening to the majestic song "The Holy City" at the moment when the elevated City of David first appeared to us. It was a breathtaking moment for all of us, especially for those who were seeing Jerusalem for the first time.

If we expect to receive the blessings of worship enumerated in Psalm 84:5–12, we must be willing to make the necessary preparation described in the first four verses.

That is the kind of experience that the psalmist had each time he approached the "dwelling place" of God (Ps. 84:1). For the Israelites, God uniquely dwelled in the temple that Solomon had built in Jerusalem (Deuteronomy 12:5; 2 Chronicles 6:1–2; 7:1–3). The most sacred piece of worship furniture associated with the presence of God, the ark of the covenant, was placed in the most holy room of the temple. The temple was a special place because of its association with the presence of God. Jesus reminded the woman at Jacob's well and us that the presence of God is more important than the place (John 4:19–24), however.

When the psalmist saw the temple, he felt sheer joy. It was a significant place to him because of the Person of God whom he felt in that place. Christ's followers should approach the worship experience in this way. Corporate worship concerns a mighty Person and a meaningful place. Do you rejoice in the privilege of coming into the presence of the sovereign God in a place where attention will be focused on him?

. . . The worshiper receives spiritual benefit from being in the presence of God with others.

The Israelites used the phrase "LORD Almighty" (Ps. 84:1, 3, 8, and 12) to emphasize the power of Yahweh. The term emphasized the sovereignty of God over all beings and God's authority over his enemies.

Verse 2 is yet another instructive example of Hebrew parallelism in poetry. Each part of the verse has a similar counterpart. "Soul" is the word *nephesh*, a term that denotes the totality of one's being, while "heart" and "flesh" signify the internal attitudes and the external physicality. The psalmist sought to experience God with the entirety of his being, including his thoughts, his emotions, and his will.

The association of "courts of the LORD" with "the living God" shows that the magnetic power of the place resulted from the personal God whom the psalmist would encounter in that place. This worshiper did not approach God in an apathetic or lazy way. The worshiper came alert and prepared to meet God. I am afraid that often we do not approach times of worship with that kind of attitude. We may not be as prepared and alert to experience the presence of the true and living God as was this psalmist.

The psalmist envied those who were able to spend more time in the temple area than he did. It may be that he saw birds that had built their nests in the stone crevices of the building or that occupied trees in the courtyard area (84:3). The psalmist felt as much at home in God's house as these creatures that actually lived there. In the same way, he envied the priests and other servants who had the privilege of living in the temple precinct (84:4). He felt the presence of God so strongly that he ideally felt that it would be wonderful to live or dwell there. (His idea could certainly be debated by clergy or laypeople who find themselves essentially "living" at the church.) He pined for more time to engage God in worship, not for more time to attend committee meetings or carry out administrative duties.

. . . When we encounter God in worship, we are "blessed" (84:5).

The psalmist is a positive role model for the appropriate way to prepare for worship experiences. We should see the worship place and opportunity as a "lovely" place (84:1). We should desire rather than dread times of worship. We should rejoice in our times of worship, wishing they could be extended rather than shortened.

Worship leaders certainly have responsibilities in prayerfully planning experiences that will be meaningful to us, but worshipers have preparation responsibilities as well. On occasion the sermon may not be inspiring. The music may not be your preference in worship style. But, even if the elements of worship are not perfectly implemented, you are the most important person in determining the benefits and blessings you receive from worship.

We need to worship God with others because of the reciprocal or mutual strength or encouragement that we receive.

Zion

Zion originally denoted the fortified hill that protected the pre-Israelite city of Jerusalem. It was a strong fortification that the Jebusites continued to control through the Israelite periods of conquest and judges. David conquered it with his personal militia (2 Samuel 5:6–10). He made Zion (Jerusalem) his capital city, or "the City of David" (2 Sam. 5:9).

The psalmists frequently referred to the temple of Solomon as Zion (Ps. 2:6; 48:2; 84:7; 132:13). In these worship contexts, Zion denoted the triumphant or sovereign rule of God, who would vanquish all of Israel's enemies. Possibly the placement of the ark of the covenant (associated with the might or rule of God) within the temple initiated this association. The prophets used the term Zion when they described the city of God in the new age (Isaiah 1:27; 28:16; 33:5). New Testament writers spoke of the heavenly city as Zion (Hebrews 12:22; Revelation 14:1). The term Zion retains a confident and triumphant spirit in Christian music in hymns like "We're Marching to Zion."[1]

Reflection

Scan this list of factors that may enhance or distract from one's potential for genuine worship. Prioritize them in the order of their importance in contributing to *your* meaningful times of worship.

- The number of distractions and disturbances by others
- The beauty and comfort level of the worship center
- The quality of the musicians and preacher
- The crisis issues or relationships in life that I am dealing with
- The presence of areas of unconfessed disobedience in my life
- Thoughtful reflection and preparation prior to the service

Questions

1. What is the purpose of worship?

2. Name as many obstacles as you can to the successful accomplishment of your responses to the first question. What can worship leaders or worshipers do to overcome those obstacles?

3. What do you do each week to prepare your own heart for worship? What could you do to improve your preparation?

4. What advice could worship participants offer to worship planners?

5. Outline an order of service for the ideal worship experience. Design the various elements and explain the desired flow of the service.

NOTES

1. Words by Isaac Watts.

Focal Text

Psalm 90

Background

Psalm 90

Main Idea

Even though our lives are brief and may be troubled, we can experience joy and meaning when we turn in faith to God.

Question to Explore

Where can we find meaning in this all too brief life and the predicaments in which we sometimes find ourselves?

LESSON SEVEN To Live a Life That Matters

Study Aim

To identify implications for my life from the psalmist's concerns about life as well as from how the psalmist found a meaningful life in spite of these concerns

Study and Action Emphases

- Affirm the Bible as our authoritative guide for life and ministry
- Share the gospel with all people
- Develop a growing, vibrant faith

Quick Read

In contrast to an eternal and holy God, human experience is both temporary and sinful. In spite of that, we can enjoy a meaningful life if we trust in God.

Last year my wife and I received a letter from a former neighbor who was then a stay-at-home mom but is now a Methodist minister. She had written the note as a devotional assignment. The letter blessed us. Let me share it with you:

> I want to share the story of when I lived in Pasadena, Texas, across the street from a pastor and his family. Ron and Brenda had four kids, three boys and a girl. In the twelve years that Tony and I lived there, we watched a huge range of growth in the kids. Little did this family know of the impact they were having on me as I watched their lives in the coming and going of my own life. The one thing that still penetrates my soul today was the purity and innocence radiated by each child. Quietly my heart yearned for my life and my children's lives to yield such a glow. Ron and Brenda still don't know how their daily witness blessed and directed my life.

Psalm 90 is the same kind of testimony letter as the one Marianne sent to us. It reminds us that although human life is brief and characterized by unfaithfulness to God, our trust in God really can make a difference in our influence on others.

Psalm 90 begins the fourth section, Book IV, in the Book of Psalms. Its placement here seems to have been intentional. Book III contains a number of prayers lamenting the destruction of Jerusalem. The final psalm in that section (Psalm 89) concerns God's rejection of the dynasty of Davidic kings. That rejection raises the question of what that might mean for Israel.

Psalm 90 and the section that it begins provide the answer to that question. God will continue to work with his people because he had made a covenant with them through his servant Moses. We find a reference to Moses in the title to Psalm 90 and six other times in this section (Ps. 99:6; 103:7; 105:26; 106:16, 23, 32). Compare that to only one other reference to Moses outside of Book IV (77:21).

How should we understand the reference to Moses in the superscription? Moses may have written it, but that is not likely. It is more probable that the Israelites associated Moses with this psalm because of its theme and language. Moses lived a long life and yet did not seemingly complete his mission as he failed to lead the Israelites into the Promised Land. He, therefore, provided the logical example of the "cut short" nature, or brief and temporary experience, of human life. In addition, this psalm contains some of the thought and language of the dialogue between God and Moses in Exodus 32—34 (see Ps. 90:13).

Old Testament interpreters have been divided over how to classify this psalm. Some consider it to be a community lament. That would signify the presence of a complaint to God regarding the difficulty of life and a request for his help. It certainly has the form of a prayer as the psalmist addressed God, but it lacks any specifics as to a source of the complaint. Other interpreters suggest that it is a wisdom poem. If that is so, it would not be a complaint against God; rather, it would simply be instruction or a statement about the basic nature of human life.

Psalm 90

1 Lord, you have been our dwelling place
throughout all generations.
2 Before the mountains were born
or you brought forth the earth and the world,
from everlasting to everlasting you are God.
3 You turn men back to dust,
saying, "Return to dust, O sons of men."
4 For a thousand years in your sight
are like a day that has just gone by,
or like a watch in the night.
5 You sweep men away in the sleep of death;
they are like the new grass of the morning—
6 though in the morning it springs up new,
by evening it is dry and withered.
7 We are consumed by your anger
and terrified by your indignation.
8 You have set our iniquities before you,
our secret sins in the light of your presence.
9 All our days pass away under your wrath;
we finish our years with a moan.

10 The length of our days is seventy years—
or eighty, if we have the strength;
yet their span is but trouble and sorrow,
for they quickly pass, and we fly away.
11 Who knows the power of your anger?
For your wrath is as great as the fear that is due
you.
12 Teach us to number our days aright,
that we may gain a heart of wisdom.
13 Relent, O LORD! How long will it be?
Have compassion on your servants.
14 Satisfy us in the morning with your unfailing love,
that we may sing for joy and be glad all our days.
15 Make us glad for as many days as you have
afflicted us,
for as many years as we have seen trouble.
16 May your deeds be shown to your servants,
your splendor to their children.
17 May the favor of the Lord our God rest upon us;
establish the work of our hands for us—
yes, establish the work of our hands.

Praise to the Eternal God (90:1–2)

A focus on God at the beginning of this psalm is both intentional and important. Living a life that matters has to do with relating one's life to God. It is only in light of who God is and what God desires for us that we can entertain the idea of a "purpose-driven life."

We cannot comprehend human existence apart from the One who made us. The psalmist made three statements about God in verses 1–2.

First, he declared that God provided help, security, or refuge for his people. The word underlying "dwelling place" (90:1) often referred to the habitations or dens where animals lived (Jeremiah 10:22; 49:33). It signified a home, a place of refuge or security. Each and every generation experienced the comfort of the security of God.

The God who is our security is the God who made everything and was God even before he did that work.

Second, the psalmist then emphasized the work of God as the Creator of the world in which we live. The verbs of verse 2, "born" and "brought forth," are the ones commonly used to describe the labor pain or travail associated with the birth process.

Third, the psalmist then made sure that the reader understood the significant distinction between the One who created everything and that which was created. God was not created and, therefore, does not share in the time and space limitations of things and people he created. He existed "before" everything was born; that is, he had no birth or beginning. The language "from everlasting to everlasting" (Ps. 90:2) declares the eternal or timeless dimension of God's nature. The God who is our security is the God who made everything and was God even before he did that work.

The Shortness of Human Life (90:3–6)

"Time flies" is how we express it. We live at a hectic pace. We desire to squeeze every small meaning or use out of our time. We are a fast food, express lane, microwave culture. Every business person knows the importance of speed in meeting the demands of customers and thereby achieving success. Maybe no generation before us has been as time conscious as ours is.

The psalmist drew an impressive contrast between the eternal God and humankind, who know the challenge of being time limited by time. Our lives have a beginning and an end. The psalmist graphically portrayed the reality of the latter. "Dust" (90:3) is not simply the word for the physical component of human existence; rather, it denoted something that was crushed or pulverized. Maybe when we are "pressed for time," we subconsciously anticipate the crushing end to which we will all submit. The fact that we are created contains inherently a mortality factor. All "sons of men" (90:3) will return to dust. "Men" is the Hebrew word *adam* (the first of the species), who was created from the *adamah* (ground).

> *The speed at which grass lived and died reminded the psalmist of the shortness of human existence.*

Since humanity is severely limited by time, we segment it or mark it. A millennium, a thousand years, is an extremely long period of time to us (90:4).

It possesses no such connotation with God. It may not be entirely appropriate to say that time means nothing to God, for our time (what we do with it) does matter to him. Maybe we should say that it does not have the same meaning or effect on God as it does on us. The reason for that is that a thousand years to God is like a single day or a "watch in the night" (90:4). This expression described the shortest measurement of time known to the first hearers of this psalm.

Living a life that matters has to do with relating one's life to God.

Our lives come and go as rapidly as the grass. The psalmist observed that the grass nourished by the moisture of the morning dew looked promising. By the end of the day, though, it had experienced the devastation of the burning sun, and it withered away. The speed at which grass lived and died reminded the psalmist of the shortness of human existence. Jesus would also use the life span of flowers and grass, but he used it to teach a different lesson (Matthew 6:28–30).

The Sinfulness of Human Life (90:7–11)

Our lives are not only limited by time but are characterized by radical disobedience against God. These verses reveal a clear progression. God is fully aware of human sinfulness (90:8). Our sins cause anger to God and misery to us (Ps. 90:7, 9). Sin, as well as the resultant trouble that it causes, is prevalent throughout our lives (90:10).

Interpreters debate whether the psalmist expressed himself in an excessively gloomy and pessimistic way or in a realistic and honest way. What he did declare is what each of us knows to be the truth. All of us have failed to live up to God's standards for our lives. We have all sinned against God (Romans 3:23). "The light of your presence" (Ps. 90:8) is literally *the lamp of your face*. Think of the dreadful appearance of our sins as the holy nature of God shines brightly on them.

Our sins have an impact on God. While we should be careful when we speak about the anger of God, we should not be reluctant to speak about it, for it is part of the biblical witness. The psalmist used three words in verses 7, 9, and 11 to describe God's response to human sin, and the New International Version appropriately renders them with three different English words. "Anger" (90:7, 11) is the Hebrew word for *nose* or *nostril*. The Hebrews observed that when one became angry, the nose dilated, and the person took short breaths. As a result they utilized the term for this body part to describe the emotion of displeasure. This word thus emphasized the emotional aspects of anger. Our sins cause God to feel pained, wounded, and greatly displeased. His anger is fierce but not evil.

In order to depend on God's guidance, we must allow him to deal with our sinful nature.

The word "indignation" (90:7) was derived from the verbal root meaning *to be warmed* or *hot*. The word signified something that was physically warmed or, as here, someone who was emotionally hot or furious.

"Wrath" (90:9, 11), a synonym for "anger," emphasizes the terrifying result of God's response to sin. This word declares that God's anger is fierce, completely overwhelming, and cannot be avoided as to its consequences. The verb rendered "consumed" (90:7) and "finish" (90:9) confirms that truth, for it has the sense of bringing something to a full or final completion.

Our sins cause God to feel pained, wounded, and greatly displeased.

As a result of God's displeasure we end our lives with a "moan" (90:9), a brief sigh of resignation or weariness. The length of our life does not matter. A life span of seventy or eighty years (considerably beyond their life expectancy rather than the standard to be expected) simply means that we will experience more trouble and sadness. "Fly away" (90:10) denotes a wishful longing to escape the oppressive nature of human life.

Prayer to the Eternal God (90:12–17)

The time for gloomy pessimism has passed. The eternal God, the psalmist's "dwelling place" (90:1), is the only One capable of helping the psalmist confront his temporary and sinful life. The psalmist maintains his fear or reverence (respect) for God.

Verse 12 serves as the transitional verse in this psalm. Psalm 90:1–11 contains descriptive statements concerning what the psalmist realized. Verses 12–17 contain imperatives or requests that he made to God based on these realizations. The psalmist recognized our inability to make life matter apart from God; therefore, we need God to instruct us in the way to live our lives wisely. We may use the expression "your days are numbered" in a threatening way, but that is not the sense here. We do not need God to help us to count our days but to make our days count. Our days count when we depend on God to guide our decisions and behavior.

In order to depend on God's guidance, we must allow him to deal with our sinful nature. The psalmist, therefore, asked God to "relent" (90:13). The Hebrew word here, *shub*, is the common word for the human experience of the repentance of sins (a turning back or turning around). God has no need to repent of any wrongdoing, for God commits no sin. Here the psalmist asked God to turn back from the expression of his anger and wrath. That meaning is confirmed by the verb that is in a parallel position to *shub*. "Have compassion" (90:13b) is quite a significant word in the Old Testament. (See the article, "The Turning of God.") The psalmist

We do not need God to help us to count our days but to make our days count.

asked God to turn back or to change his course of action.

The basis for this honest request was the "unfailing love" (90:14) of God. If God would express his loyal and faithful love or loving-kindness to his people, then they would experience joy and gladness for all of their lives instead of enduring God's wrath. The psalmist realized that they did not deserve a formal settling of accounts or justice (the equal number of days of joy to compensate for the days of anger); rather, they simply would be grateful to God for his mercy (90:15).

Our days count when we depend on God to guide our decisions and behavior.

How would the psalmist know whether God had changed his stance toward them or not? The grace or favor of God would be revealed in the productivity and accomplishment of human work (90:17) and in the blessing on future generations (90:16). When we receive affirmations about our children, that helps us conclude that living a life of faithfulness to God really does matter. That was the assurance of Marianne's letter.

The Turning of God

"Have compassion" (Ps. 90:13) translates the Hebrew word *naham*. Its root meaning is *to feel sorrow over something* or *to feel sorry for someone*. Sometimes God felt sorrow to the extent that he desired to bring comfort (Isaiah 40:1; Ps. 23:4). At other times God had such sadness that he determined to act in a different way. In essence God changed his plan (but not his nature).

In the time of Noah, God expressed sorrow over the sinfulness of his created beings and determined to bring great destruction (Genesis 6:6–7). When God determined to destroy the Israelites for constructing an idol at Sinai, Moses asked God to change his mind (Exodus 32:12). The psalmist here requested God to do just that, to change his posture toward him. He wanted God to turn from anger to mercy. He did not ask God to reverse life's brevity or mortality. He asked God to reverse human sinfulness (by choosing to forgive).

Reflection

Evaluate the following statements on the basis of whether they are *1*—very important; *2*—somewhat important; *3*—neutral; *4*—not important at all in helping someone live a life that matters:

- The amount of material resources one has
- The use of each day to help other people
- The number of people who know who you are
- A reverence for the everlasting God
- The level of involvement in one's church
- The presence or absence of a spouse and children

- Willingness to confess sinfulness to God
- The setting where you live—rural, suburban, or urban area

Questions

1. What criteria must be present to describe someone's passing as an "untimely death"?

2. What do you think of first when you hear the phrase "the anger of God"? What troubles you about this concept? What reassures you about this concept?

3. What are practical things that you do that help you make every day count in your faithfulness to God and others?

4. What testimony letter could you write to someone who has made a big difference in your relationship to God? What keeps you from writing it?

LESSON EIGHT

Praise for God's Goodness

Focal Text

Psalms 100; 103

Background

Psalms 100; 103; 105

Main Idea

Praise God for God's goodness to us, shown in so many ways.

Question to Explore

In what ways has God shown his goodness to you?

Study Aim

To identify specific ways God has shown his goodness to me and to offer praise to God

Study and Action Emphases

- Affirm the Bible as our authoritative guide for life and ministry
- Share the gospel with all people
- Develop a growing, vibrant faith

Quick Read

God demonstrates his goodness to us in a variety of ways. Our recognition and acknowledgement of that goodness should return to God in praise.

Without the assistance of a Google search or the help of an encyclopedia, what do you know about Thomas Ken? The probability is great that you have sung his words (maybe hundreds of times). I will provide some clues to his identity. He was a leader of the Anglican church in seventeenth-century England (1637–1711). He became a bishop at Bath, the place where people had come to receive the healing therapy of the natural hot springs since the Roman period. He spent some time imprisoned in the Tower of London because he refused to sign King James II's Declaration of Indulgence that sought to return England to the Roman Catholic Church.

I know. None of that information seems relevant to you. What I want you to know, however, is that most of us have used his words to express praise to our God. We have taken his words as our own expression of adoration to God, for Thomas Ken is the author of what is popularly known as the "Doxology."[1] His words invite us to offer praise to God, the source of all blessings. We sing his words to a tune designated as "Old 100th." The tune was so named because it was first applied to a poem based on Psalm 100.

For centuries of Christian history, Christ's followers have used the words of others to express our praise and worship to God. Before the acceptance and popularity of Christian hymn writers like Thomas Ken, Christ's followers (as Jewish worshipers before them) almost exclusively used the poems from the Book of Psalms for this purpose.

Review the information in the introductory article, "Introducing the Book of Psalms: Songs of Faith," about the five major types or kinds of psalms that we find in the Book of Psalms. One of them is hymns of praise. In fact, about half of the poems in the book are in this category (74 of 150). Psalms 100, 103, and 105 are all hymns of praise. These poems generally speak about God in the third person rather than in second-person direct address.

The hymns of praise follow a well-defined structure (with variations in the length of each component). They begin with an invitation (or command) to offer praise to God. They then provide the basis or rationale for that invitation. This declarative statement of the nature or actions of God explains why it is appropriate to praise God. The praise hymns conclude with a final reminder (invitation) to praise God.

Apply this outline to Psalm 105. The psalmist invites us to praise God (Psalm 105:1–6). He justifies that praise due to the grace God had extended to the Israelites first during the patriarchal period (Ps. 105:7–22) and also during the period of the Exodus from Egypt (105:23–45a). He then reminds us to praise God (105:45b). Before you read the additional comments here, read and apply this outline pattern to Psalms 100 and 103.

Psalm 100

1 Shout for joy to the LORD, all the earth.
2 Worship the LORD with gladness;
come before him with joyful songs.
3 Know that the LORD is God.
It is he who made us, and we are his;
we are his people, the sheep of his pasture.
4 Enter his gates with thanksgiving
and his courts with praise;
give thanks to him and praise his name.
5 For the LORD is good and his love endures forever;
his faithfulness continues through all
generations.

Psalm 103

1 Praise the LORD, O my soul;
all my inmost being, praise his holy name.
2 Praise the LORD, O my soul,
and forget not all his benefits—
3 who forgives all your sins
and heals all your diseases,
4 who redeems your life from the pit
and crowns you with love and compassion,
5 who satisfies your desires with good things
so that your youth is renewed like the eagle's.
6 The LORD works righteousness
and justice for all the oppressed.

7 He made known his ways to Moses,
his deeds to the people of Israel:
8 The LORD is compassionate and gracious,
slow to anger, abounding in love.
9 He will not always accuse,
nor will he harbor his anger forever;
10 he does not treat us as our sins deserve
or repay us according to our iniquities.
11 For as high as the heavens are above the earth,
so great is his love for those who fear him;
12 as far as the east is from the west,
so far has he removed our transgressions from us.
13 As a father has compassion on his children,
so the LORD has compassion on those who fear him;
14 for he knows how we are formed,
he remembers that we are dust.
15 As for man, his days are like grass,
he flourishes like a flower of the field;
16 the wind blows over it and it is gone,
and its place remembers it no more.
17 But from everlasting to everlasting
the LORD's love is with those who fear him,
and his righteousness with their children's children—
18 with those who keep his covenant
and remember to obey his precepts.
19 The LORD has established his throne in heaven,
and his kingdom rules over all.

20 Praise the LORD, you his angels,
you mighty ones who do his bidding,
who obey his word.
21 Praise the LORD, all his heavenly hosts,
you his servants who do his will.
22 Praise the LORD, all his works
everywhere in his dominion.
Praise the LORD, O my soul.

The Invitation to Praise God (100:1–4; 103:1–2)

As classic hymns of praise, both psalms begin with an invitation to praise God characterized by the use of imperative verb forms. Psalm 103 is the more personal and individualistic of the two psalms. This psalmist encouraged himself to recognize the goodness of God. "Soul" (Ps. 103:1, 2) denotes the entire being made possible by the breath of God (Genesis 2:7).

"Praise" (Ps. 103:1, 2) translates the Hebrew root *barak*, usually translated as either "praise" (NIV) or "bless" (NRSV, NASB, KJV). The basic meaning refers to something done for someone by one who is recognized to be in a superior position. The reference could be to enabling someone to achieve power, success, or prosperity. Historically related to the word meaning *knee*, it denoted the bending of the knee or bowing when receiving a word or deed from a superior. The Scripture affirms that God

Our lives begin and end in God.

is the only source for blessing. When we receive such blessing (*barak*) from God, we should praise (*barak*) him. The use of the same word for what God does and what we do in recognition of what he does affirms their close connection.

In contrast to the introspective individualism of Psalm 103, Psalm 100 invites "all the earth" (100:1) to join in praising God for his goodness. The invitation to praise God dominates Psalm 100 (four of the five verses). Psalm 100 contains seven imperative verb forms or commands.

The command in the center of the seven is the unique one and thus the foundational one. While the other six describe an action to be taken, this one involves something to affirm or know. Praise of God begins with our understanding of who God is. "Know that the LORD is God" (100:3), the recognition that Yahweh is the one and only living God, is the basic affirmation of Israelite faith (Deut. 4:35, 39; 6:4; 1 Kings 18:39). Our lives begin and end in God. We are God's by right of creation and elective grace. "Made" (Ps. 100:3) was used both for God's acts in creation and for his work in creating Israel to be his people.

. . . God is the source of all blessings, both material and spiritual.

The six other commands are actions that should naturally result from our recognition of the sovereignty of God. We use the phrase "serve the LORD" (100:2) frequently, but it is a rare phrase in the Book of Psalms (only here and 2:11). The word translated "serve" has a wide range of meaning. It referred to the work of a slave, a soldier, or a citizen subject. The common factor is the recognition of allegiance due to a superior (master, commander, king). Serving God thus meant to acknowledge that one belonged to God (our Master, Commander, and King). It also referred to the periodic public recognition of God's sovereignty (worship).

"Shout for joy" (100:1) signified the noisy acclaim for the king when his subjects first saw him. "Come" (100:2) and "enter" (100:4) translate the same Hebrew word. It generally meant *to draw near*, but it was also a technical term for the respectful approach to a king.

The final two commands in the invitation are "give thanks" and "praise" (100:4) This verse provides another clear example of the parallelism in Hebrew poetry ("gates"/"courts" and "thanksgiving"/"praise"; see lesson one article, "Hebrew Poetry and Parallelism"). "Praise" is the same word found in Psalm 103:1–2. The discussion of Psalm 116 in next week's study will contain the background and significance of the terminology of "thanksgiving" (100:4).

The Explanation of God's Goodness (100:5; 103:3–19)

Every worshiper should appreciate the explanation that the author of Psalm 100 provided in verse 5.

Note its brevity, its simplicity, and yet its majesty. The verse contains three key terms. This is the only time in the Old Testament in which all three appear together in this form. They declare that God is the source of all blessings, both material and spiritual.

> *The psalmist was grateful for the reality of his spiritual healing before he acknowledged whatever physical healing he had experienced.*

"Good" (100:5) is the designation of approval for all of God's creative work (Gen. 1:4, 10, 12, 18, 21, 25, 31). The Lord created everything that exists, and he shares material or physical blessings with us out of the world that he makes available to us.

"Love" (Ps. 100:5) denotes Yahweh's promise to be faithful forever to the covenant relationship that he established with Israel at Sinai (also 90:14; Hebrew, *hesed*). God voluntarily obligated himself to his creation, and he is fully committed to fulfill that obligation. The words referring to the goodness and the faithful love of God are also linked in Psalm 23:6.

The last word in this trilogy is "faithfulness" (*emunah*). It is constructed from the verbal root *to be firm or reliable.* From this word we get the English word *amen*, denoting that we agree that something we heard is reliable, dependable. This word occurs no less than seven times in Psalm 89, which laments the fall of the Davidic king. In spite of the end of an earthly dynasty, God would continue to be the dependable partner of his people.

Browse verses 1–17 in Psalm 103, noticing the many examples of Hebrew poetic parallelism. These verses are impressive in their artistry in the use of word pairs, synonyms, and contrasts.

The psalmist shared his explanation of God's goodness from the inside out. The psalmist's invitation was an encouragement to himself to praise God, and so he began by asserting what God had done for him (103:3–5). Admirably the psalmist began his list with spiritual blessings instead of material or physical blessings. How many times do we begin our praise with the abundant material gifts of God rather than with the gift of salvation and the advantage that grows out of that relationship? The psalmist was grateful for the reality of his spiritual healing before he acknowledged whatever physical healing he had experienced. The strength of renewal (103:5) is close to the "born again" image of the New Testament.

The limitless extent of God's love makes possible the removal of sins to a distance we cannot understand (103:11–12).

"Love" (103:4), an important word in this psalm (also 103:8, 11, 17), translates the word *hesed*, which describes God's faithful or loyal love. "Compassion" (103:4), another important word here (also 103:8, 13), is found frequently with *hesed* (love, loving-kindness). "Compassion" describes the tender love of parents toward their children, coming from the word for a woman's womb.

The psalmist recognized that God had blessed the community of faith as well (103:6–13). He addressed the tension between what God willed or desired and what God chose to do when his people did not obey God's will. "Justice" and "righteousness" (103:6) denote what God desired. This word pair, found frequently in the Book of Psalms (9:7–8; 89:14; 97:2) and in the prophets (see Isaiah 5:7), spoke of God's living up to his covenant responsibilities (including judgment) and his fair and impartial rule.

No one and no thing is beyond the sovereignty of God (103:19).

We feel the tension between the demands of God's rightness and justice over against God's loyal love and tender mercy. It is the antithetical pull toward just punishment and undeserved forgiveness.

One of the clearest illustrations of that tension comes from the narrative of Exodus 32—34, when God established the Sinai covenant agreement with Israel. While Moses received the Ten Words from God on the mountain, the people were constructing their golden calf idol in the valley. God declared his intention to destroy the people completely. God would have done that except for the tender, compassionate side of God's nature. Psalm 103:8–10 reflects that Sinai incident. In fact, each of the attributes of God in verse 8 is found in the significant description of God in Exodus 34:6–7. God does get angry concerning our sins, but he has determined to forgive them.

The limitless extent of God's love makes possible the removal of sins to a distance we cannot understand (Ps. 103:11–12).

The psalmist broadened his perspective even more. He began with himself and expanded to include the faith community. Beyond that, God has blessed the totality of created humanity (103:15–18).

God is fully aware of our human creatureliness and frailty. We hear echoes of Psalm 90 in the contrast between our time-limited existence and the eternality of God. No one and no thing is beyond the sovereignty of God (103:19).

The Affirmation of God's Creation (103:20–22)

Any serious understanding of human transience should elicit from us two important reactions. One is the appreciation that God is near and available to us. We can thus know God through his love, compassion, and forgiveness. The psalmist has emphasized these things (103:3–5, 6–13, 17). The other reaction is the appreciation of the immensity or the transcendence of God. The psalmist addresses that aspect in verses 20–22.

. . . God is near and available to us.

Conclusions to hymns of praise return to the invitation in form and sentiment. Since verse 19 has declared that Yahweh's kingdom extends to the entire universe, it is appropriate for the psalmist to invite the entire creation to praise God (see 103:20–22). That means that spiritual beings are as obligated to praise God as are physical or human beings.

Even as an earthly king was surrounded by a large number of royal servants whose priority purpose was to serve his needs, the eternal King enjoys the presence of spiritual helpers. "Angels" (103:20) emphasizes the messenger role of these beings; they serve as intermediaries between heaven and earth. "Heavenly hosts" (103:21) represents the word translated "hosts" in the phrase *Lord of hosts*, or "LORD Almighty" (84:12).

It is quite easy to be so overwhelmed with the immensity of God that we feel "lost in the shuffle." Perhaps we think, *If God receives the praise of the vast universe, what possible difference could my small and insignificant praise make?* I do not know fully what difference it might make to God, but I do know that it makes a large difference to us. That is why the psalmist began where he started. He encouraged himself to join the entire universe in giving praise to God.

Ogbomosho

Ogbomosho is in Yoruba land in southwestern Nigeria, a country with significant numbers of Baptist Christians. T. J. Bowen and his wife represent the first Baptist presence in Nigeria, arriving there in 1850. Ogbomosho was among the earliest locations of Baptist work in Nigeria. A monument of Bowen stands in a church courtyard there. Charles and Cynthia Morris also labored there (1884–1889). It was hard work.

The Nigerian Baptist Theological Seminary was established at Ogbomosho in 1898. When it celebrated its centennial in 1998, John Mills, a Texan, former missionary in Nigeria, and retired coordinator for all of West Africa, delivered the keynote address. Currently that seminary enjoys a partnership with Texas Baptists. Professors from the Logsdon School of Theology and the University of Mary Hardin-Baylor have been guest professors for mini-semesters there.

When the W. J. Davids arrived in Ogbomosho in 1877–78 to restore a discontinued work, the people asserted, "God be praised! He has heard our prayers which continued these many years." In spite of difficulty, God is good and worthy of our praise.

Questions

1. Read Psalms 134; 135; and 136 (three hymns of praise) and see whether they follow the typical structure of these kinds of poems.

2. Reading hymns of praise allows us to express praise through the words of others. What song that Christians sing today has words that help you praise God?

3. How many times do you find the word "all" in Psalm 103? What do you think might be the significance of that?

4. How has God been good to you? Make a list of five to ten things God has done for you.

5. Look at the list you have made. Has God's goodness been more in the form of blessing or in the form of strength to endure difficult circumstances?

6. To what family member or friend do you most often express your praise of God?

NOTES

1. "Praise God, from Whom All Blessings Flow."

LESSON NINE

Give Thanks for God's Blessings

Focal Text

Psalm 116

Background

Psalms 107; 116

Main Idea

God's blessings in time of dire need call for acts of sincere thanksgiving.

Question to Explore

How will you say *thank you* to God?

Study Aim

To decide on ways I will give thanks to God for God's blessings

Study and Action Emphases

- Affirm the Bible as our authoritative guide for life and ministry
- Develop a growing, vibrant faith

Quick Read

Expressing thanks does not come naturally for the human species. It is a learned behavior. Followers of Christ should seek to improve the quality of their expressions of gratitude to God.

What is the source of a thankful spirit, one that regularly expresses gratitude, including to God? We are certainly not genetically coded to be people of thanksgiving. If that were the case, we would never hear parents coach their precious little ones with *What do you say?* after the child has received a gift. Thanksgiving is an attitude and action that we have to learn or develop. This study can help us do that.

Songs of thanksgiving is another of the types of poems that comprise the Book of Psalms (see the article at the beginning of this study, "Introducing the Book of Psalms: Songs of Faith"). A thanksgiving song was an expression of thanksgiving to God for graciously providing deliverance.

We detect two types of thanksgiving songs in the book. Community thanksgiving songs rejoice in the way God responded to a desperate need experienced by his people (military threats or economic devastation). Individual thanksgiving songs rejoiced in the way God responded to a need in one person's life (physical illness, opposition or oppression, ridicule or rejection, persecution). I believe that songs of individual thanksgiving played a role for the Israelites similar to the one played by Christian testimonies today (see the small article, "Christian Testimony").

Songs of thanksgiving have a typical structure but also demonstrate quite a creative variety. Such a psalm generally begins with an expression of praise and gratitude to God. The psalm then describes the trouble or distress that the psalmist (or the psalmist's community) experienced and that caused him to plead with God for help. The psalmist then declares that God delivered him or the community from the desperate situation. As a result he would offer the appropriate sacrifice and testify to the saving work of God in order to encourage others. Encouraging others is a reason we share our spiritual testimonies today.

This lesson considers songs of thanksgiving by focusing on Psalm 116, with Psalm 107 in the background Scripture. Some identify Psalm 107 as a community thanksgiving song, and some consider it to be an individual thanksgiving song. Even if it is an individual thanksgiving song, it was probably used by the community because it includes the characteristic elements of the community thanksgiving type. It celebrates the faithful or loyal love of God (Psalm 107:1, 43). The psalmist offered illustrations of how God had graciously shared his loyal love with people in various states of need, declaring that the people whom God had thus blessed should give thanks to God. The various illustrations can be identified by the repeated statement, "Let them give thanks to the Lord for his unfailing love" (Ps.107:8, 15, 21, 31).

Psalm 116 is one of the individual thanksgiving songs (see also 30; 34; 92; 118). The songs of thanksgiving were closely associated with the laments (also individual and community) in content and form. Laments describe present situations, while thanksgiving songs are laments about some distress in the past along with the declaration of thanksgiving because God had already provided deliverance. Sometimes it is difficult to determine whether a psalm should be understood as a lament or a song of thanksgiving because of the verb forms in the poem.

Psalm 116

1 I love the Lord, for he heard my voice;
he heard my cry for mercy.
2 Because he turned his ear to me,
I will call on him as long as I live.
3 The cords of death entangled me,
the anguish of the grave came upon me;
I was overcome by trouble and sorrow.
4 Then I called on the name of the Lord:
"O Lord, save me!"
5 The Lord is gracious and righteous;
our God is full of compassion.
6 The Lord protects the simplehearted;
when I was in great need, he saved me.
7 Be at rest once more, O my soul,
for the Lord has been good to you.
8 For you, O Lord, have delivered my soul from death,
my eyes from tears,
my feet from stumbling,
9 that I may walk before the Lord
in the land of the living.

10 I believed; therefore I said,
"I am greatly afflicted."
11 And in my dismay I said,
"All men are liars."
12 How can I repay the LORD
for all his goodness to me?
13 I will lift up the cup of salvation
and call on the name of the LORD.
14 I will fulfill my vows to the LORD
in the presence of all his people.
15 Precious in the sight of the LORD
is the death of his saints.
16 O LORD, truly I am your servant;
I am your servant, the son of your maidservant;
you have freed me from my chains.
17 I will sacrifice a thank offering to you
and call on the name of the LORD.
18 I will fulfill my vows to the LORD
in the presence of all his people,
19 in the courts of the house of the LORD—
in your midst, O Jerusalem.
Praise the LORD.

Where Does Thanksgiving Come From? (116:1–7)

Thanksgiving to God grows out of our relationship to him. We are willing to express gratitude to God because we love him and realize that he has blessed our lives in so many ways. The expression "I love the

LORD" (116:1) is so familiar to us but so rare in the Book of Psalms. The only other direct parallel with this verse is Psalm 18:1, but a different word for "love" is used in that text. In Psalm 116:1 the word translated "love" is the common Hebrew word. The word refers to the voluntary and spontaneous feeling of emotional warmth and attraction to another or being kindly disposed toward another.

We are certainly not genetically coded to be people of thanksgiving.

The psalmist declared his love for God because of what God had done for him. When he was in a troubling situation, God heard his plea for help. The Hebrew verb form of "heard" (116:1) depicts incomplete action. God heard his cries in the past, and God continued to listen to him in the present when the psalmist would call to him.

Communication is an indispensable element in any relationship, especially between people who love each other. The psalmist's thanksgiving was born out of his love for God and God's willingness to be available to him.

The psalm does not contain enough information for us to identify what the psalmist's troubling situation was. The best speculation is that he suffered from some illness or disease that had caused him to be isolated from others. The language of verse 3 suggests that he possibly believed that he would not survive the disease. "Grave" (116:3) is *Sheol*, the realm of the dead. On the other hand, the psalmist may have utilized the language about death and the grave in a metaphorical way to denote a seriously threatening situation. What we do know is that the psalmist in his feeling of being overwhelmed by this trouble cried out to God. "Save me" (116:4) is literally *deliver my soul.*

Sesame Street was one of the original children's television edutainment shows. One of its vehicles used in teaching children about association of similar things was showing three or four things and then asking, "Which one of these does not belong?" Verse 5 contains three words frequently found in the Old Testament to describe an aspect of the nature of God. Two of them appear together often, but the third word rarely makes an appearance with them.

What is the source of a thankful spirit, one that regularly expresses gratitude, including to God?

"Gracious" is basic kindness, while "compassion" is the word for parental love (from the word for *womb*; see lesson eight under the heading "The Explanation of God's Goodness"). These synonyms reveal the tender, forgiving side of God. They belong together. "Righteous" translates a word that signals the faithfulness to live up to a promise or a commitment that one has made. It means doing what one says one will do. This word denotes that God made a covenant with Israel and took that commitment seriously. He will live up to that commitment, even when it means judging Israel for her unrighteousness or failure to live up to her covenant obligations. This word is usually paired with God's justice and represents the nature of God that demands the fairness of punishment of sins.

"Righteous" may not seem to belong with the words "gracious" and compassion." However, I believe all three words really do belong together. God chooses to deliver because he is kind, loves us like a model parent, and is willing to fulfill his promises to us.

May we be thankful people because of our love for God and our desire to testify to others of his work of saving grace in our lives.

On that basis God provides deliverance even for the "simple-hearted" (116:6). Although this word usually referred to someone who was naïve or willfully foolish and gullible, here it probably suggested a state of inexperience or helplessness.

The psalmist declared what God had done for him (116:6). Thus, the psalmist can rest again or be secure because of the Lord's goodness (116:7). Like the psalmist, we become thankful people when we love the Lord and rest securely in his faithful kindness and love.

What Does Thanksgiving Look Like? (116:8–14)

When we recognize what God has done and affirm our love for him, our thanksgiving will be sincere expressions of gratitude. The psalmist rejoiced in the fact that God had delivered him as he had asked (116:8). He then raised the question of how he could repay God for this good act (116:12). The question may be rhetorical. If, though, the question is to be answered, our response might be that we really cannot repay God at all. We are unable to compensate God in any meaningful or reciprocal way for God's grace.

Thanksgiving is the best way that we can make a feeble attempt to repay God for his kindness. If the psalmist repaid God with thanksgiving, what would that look like practically in his life?

- First, he determined to thank God by living an obedient life, one of integrity (116:9). If God had delivered him from death, he was going to live in a good manner.
- Second, he would couple this obedience with his faithfulness to God. The psalmist said, "I kept my faith" (116:10). Even when he suffered trouble, he remained strong in his faith. He learned that although others would betray him, God would be trustworthy (116:10–11). These verses reflect the possibility that when he needed others in his misery, they were not there for him.
- Third, since he had not been reluctant to call out to God in his trouble, he would be equally quick to call on God continuously in his expression of gratitude (116:13). He would not take his deliverance for granted. "The cup of salvation" (116:13) may refer to an element of the ritual

associated with the thank offering. Since cups of wine were a prominent part of the ceremony of Passover, this reference probably led to the connection of this psalm with the others that were sung at the beginning and end of that important feast time. These psalms are called the Hallel collection (Ps. 113—118).

- Fourth, the psalmist would show his thankfulness to God by telling others about what God had done for him. He would fulfill his ceremonial obligation in carrying out the vows or promises that he had made to God. He would ensure that the congregation knew of his gratitude (116:14).

Whom Does Thanksgiving Seek to Honor? (116:15–19)

The answer to the question in the heading is clear. Genuine thanksgiving seeks to honor God and not the individual whom God has blessed. Thanksgiving is our recognition that God has done great things. God has shown his goodness to us.

The psalmist's thanksgiving was born out of his love for God and God's willingness to be available to him.

The popular understanding of Psalm 116:15 may not reflect the original intent or meaning of the author. We sometimes hear this verse at memorial services. The preacher may comment that God receives or welcomes his children into his presence at their death. God's receiving one of his children at death is indeed a "precious" or sweet, wonderful thing to God. But is that what the psalmist would have had in mind? Remember that he had been quite vocal in asserting that God graciously delivered him from this very experience, death (116:3, 8).

I believe that we should read verses 15 and 16 together to interpret them correctly. That approach allows us to give "precious" (116:15) its most basic meaning. It denoted something that was very costly. Why would the death of a believer in God be costly to him? It is costly because it means the removal of that person's valuable service to God in this life. The psalmist recognized that God worked hard to deliver him from death; therefore, he determined to be a faithful servant as long as he lived (116:16). He would honor God through his service.

> *. . . We become thankful people when we love the Lord and rest securely in his faithful kindness and love.*

Verse 17 provides evidence for the worship context in which the Israelites used the songs of thanksgiving. "Thank offering" translates the Hebrew word *todah*, the word used both for the thanksgiving sacrificial offering and a thanksgiving action that may have substituted for the sacrifice. (For the significance of this word, see the small article, "Thanksgiving in the Old Testament.")

The thank offering was not one of the sacrifices that God required of the Israelites (Leviticus 1—7), although all sacrifices should be offered with an attitude of thanksgiving. It was rather a voluntary or free-will act that any worshiper could offer on the appropriate occasion when the worshiper desired to express gratitude to God. The instructions in Leviticus about offerings attach it to the fellowship offering (Leviticus 7:12–15).

We are unable to compensate God in any meaningful or reciprocal way for God's grace.

The psalmist pledged to worship God through his thank offering. In this public way he would seek to honor God for the great things God had done for him (Ps. 116:17–19). May we be thankful people because of our love for God and our desire to testify to others of his work of saving grace in our lives.

Christian Testimony

For many years I was ashamed of my Christian testimony. I was not ungrateful for what God had done for me in Jesus Christ, but I could not include the more exciting elements of other testimonies I heard as a teenager and young adult.

Christian parents reared me, took me to church regularly, and taught me at home about the love of God. I wanted to respond to this kind of God. I invited Jesus to become my Savior when I was six years old. My life path was pretty straight from that time. At the age of twelve I believed that God wanted to use my life in ministry. I announced that decision to my home family and my church family. I prepared myself for that kind of service. I accepted a call from the Brookston Baptist Church in northeast Texas to be their pastor when I was a junior in college. I have continued in that pastoral ministry for thirty-four years. Do you see what I mean?

So my spiritual pilgrimage did not include an extended period of willful rebellion against God and the accompanying personal misery. Then I realized that an unfaithful detour was not a necessary element of a Christian testimony. A testimony should include the circumstances of when, where, and how one came to recognize a need for Jesus; the people who may have assisted one in the decision to trust Jesus Christ as Savior and Lord; the changes that Jesus made in one's life; gratitude for what God has done; and the ways God is at work in one's life at the present time.

Thanksgiving in the Old Testament

The Hebrew language possessed no word that directly or specifically carries the meaning *to thank*. The word that is usually translated as "thank" is the Hebrew verbal root *yadah*. The primary meaning of that word is *to acknowledge or recognize something, whether it is good or bad.*

In a religious context, the Israelites used this word for the acknowledgement or confession of sin. They also used it for the recognition and declaration of the great acts of God. The confession of the character and action of God gave the word its meaning of praise.

The Hebrew understanding of thanksgiving is inseparable from the concept of the praise of God. The term then means *to confess, praise, give thanks,* or *thank.*

One form of the root of this Hebrew word is never used for a response to another human being but only to God. God's gracious actions in our behalf have no peer in human experience; therefore, the praise and gratitude we show God is in a different category from our commendation of and gratitude toward our fellow human beings.

A Question

You do not know the couple very well at all, but you were invited to the wedding. You went to the store where they had registered, and you selected something quite nice. In fact you bought something you do not even have yourself. You wrapped it in a lovely package. At the wedding, you gave it to someone who declared that she would take care of it. Two months pass. Six months pass. You received no thank-you note. What is going through your mind?

Questions

1. Forget the chicken and the egg. Which came first, love for God or gratitude?

2. What are some of the blessings of God that we tend to overlook in our thanksgiving expressions?

3. How can we repay the Lord for all of his goodness (116:12)?

4. What are the key points in your Christian testimony that could be helpful to others? (See the article, "Christian Testimony.")

Introducing

The Book of Proverbs: Sayings of Faith

The Book of Proverbs is one of three books that make up the "wisdom literature" of the Old Testament. Each of them—Job, Proverbs, and Ecclesiastes—is concerned in its own way with practical advice on how to live. Proverbs, however, takes more of a how-to approach based on traditional thinking, with Job and Ecclesiastes offering insights from another perspective. The wisdom of the Book of Proverbs is related to the Old Testament teaching that obedience to God brings blessing and disobedience brings punishment. The basic idea of the Book of Proverbs is, *If you will live like this, life will go well.*

Proverbs and "the Fear of the Lord"

All cultures have their proverbs and use proverbs to communicate generally-accepted truths in an attractive and memorable manner. English-speaking North American culture is familiar with proverbs. Think of those you know, such as these: "Haste makes waste." "The early bird gets the worm." "A stitch in time saves nine." "Waste not; want not." "A penny saved is a penny earned." "A bird in the hand is worth two in the bush." "Nothing ventured, nothing gained."

The proverbs in the Book of Proverbs are both like and unlike such secular proverbs. They have similarities to such proverbs as they communicate practical advice for living. A major difference, though, is that the Book of Proverbs is thoroughly grounded in faith in God.

Thus, although the Book of Proverbs is intensely practical, providing guidance for everyday living, it is not what we moderns would call "self-help" literature. Proverbs does call for personal response and action, but it is not the Old Testament equivalent of "self-help" literature. Proverbs 1:7, which might be called the theme or motto of the book, states plainly, "The fear of the LORD is the beginning of knowledge. . . ."[1]

Rather than compartmentalizing faith and separating it from everyday life, wisdom literature sees faith as thoroughly permeating life and offers guidance in how to apply faith in the nitty-gritty details of daily life. To do so is to put wisdom into practice.

Studying the Book of Proverbs

Several major sections are evident in the Book of Proverbs. Look in your Bible and notice these various sections:

(1) Proverbs 1—9 is introduced in Proverbs 1:1 by the words, "The proverbs of Solomon son of David, king of Israel." These chapters contain lengthier sections of similar subject matter than the remainder of the book and provide an introduction to wisdom in the Book of Proverbs.
(2) Proverbs 10:1—22:16 is introduced by the words, "The proverbs of Solomon" (Proverbs 10:1). This section contains short, pithy sayings on various topics.
(3) Proverbs 22:17—24:22 is introduced by the words, "The sayings of the wise" and refers to itself as "thirty sayings" (Prov. 22:17, 20).
(4) Proverbs 24:23–34 is introduced by the words, "These also are sayings of the wise" (24:23).
(5) Proverbs 25—29 is introduced as "more proverbs of Solomon, copied by the men of King Hezekiah of Judah" (25:1).
(6) Two brief collections conclude the Book of Proverbs. Proverbs 30 is called "the sayings of Agur son of Jakeh" (30:1), and Proverbs 31 is called "the sayings of King Lemuel—an oracle his mother taught him" (31:1).

Our study of the Book of Proverbs will deal with Scripture passages from each of these sections except the small section of sayings in Proverbs 24:23–34 and the two brief collections in Proverbs 30—31. As you study these lessons, look for how this ancient wisdom still provides practical applications to life. Recall, too, that these proverbs are based squarely on a relationship with God. That's where wisdom begins.

THE BOOK OF PROVERBS: SAYINGS OF FAITH

Lesson 10	The Beginning of Wisdom	Proverbs 1:7; 3:1–20
Lesson 11	Wisdom for Right Living	Proverbs 11:1–11, 17–21, 23–25, 28
Lesson 12	Wisdom for Every Area of Life	Proverbs 22:17–25; 23:10–11, 19–28; 24:10–12, 15–20
Lesson 13	Wisdom in Human Relationships	Proverbs 25:11–23; 26:18–28

Additional Resources for Studying the Book of Proverbs[2]

W. H. Bellinger, Jr. *The Testimony of Poets and Sages: The Psalms and Wisdom Literature.* Macon, Georgia: Smyth and Helwys Publishing, Inc., 1997.

Duane A. Garrett. "Proverbs." *The New American Commentary.* Volume 14. Nashville, Tennessee: Broadman Press, 1993.

L. D. Johnson. *Proverbs, Ecclesiastes, Song of Solomon.* Layman's Bible Book Commentary. Nashville, Tennessee: Broadman Press, 1982.

Allen P. Ross. "Proverbs." *The Expositor's Bible Commentary.* Volume 5. Grand Rapids, Michigan: Zondervan, 1991.

Marvin E. Tate, Jr. "Proverbs." *The Broadman Bible Commentary.* Volume 5. Nashville, Tennessee: Broadman Press, 1971.

Raymond C. Van Leeuwen. "Proverbs." *The New Interpreter's Bible.* Volume 5. Nashville: Abingdon Press, 1997.

NOTES

1. Unless otherwise indicated, all Scripture quotations in this article, "Introducing the Book of Proverbs: Sayings of Faith," and in the lessons on Proverbs are from the New International Version.
2. Listing a book does not imply full agreement by the writers or BAPTISTWAY PRESS® with all of its comments.

Focal Text

Proverbs 1:7; 3:1–20

Background

Proverbs 1—9

Main Idea

Following the wisdom that comes from God results in true happiness and the best kind of life.

Question to Explore

Why do people sometimes miss happiness when they pursue it so vigorously?

LESSON TEN The Beginning of Wisdom

Study Aim

To describe the wisdom that leads to the best kind of life and to make at least one application to my life

Study and Action Emphases

- Affirm the Bible as our authoritative guide for life and ministry
- Develop a growing, vibrant faith
- Equip people for servant leadership

Quick Read

Each disciple of the Lord should employ genuine wisdom, which begins in a deep sense of reverence for the majesty and holiness of the Lord.

Perhaps like you, part of my upbringing was peppered with American proverbs. Proverbs were quoted to my brother and me by my parents, grandmother, aunts and uncles, and teachers. My dad instilled this saying in me early: "A job worth doing is worth doing right the first time." To make his point, he would send me back to do a task over and to do it with more precision than I used at first.

I remember my grandmother saying, "For every stitch you take on Sunday, you will remove nine on Monday." She believed that you were not to do any work on the Lord's Day that could be done just as well on any other day. Only emergencies and necessity dictated one's activities on the Christian Sabbath.

Most proverbs I was taught were filled with the wisdom of years of experience. I accepted them as truths that would help me live better. I have found that I have repeated those same proverbs to my children and grandchildren.

Many of the proverbs that guide my life are found not only in American culture but in the Bible. My parents, grandmother, aunts and uncles, and most of my teachers were Christians. They quoted scriptural proverbs along with Southern folk proverbs. I was as apt to hear "A gentle answer turns away wrath, but a harsh word stirs up anger" (Proverbs 15:1), as I was to hear "Haste makes waste."

Proverbs 1:7

7 The fear of the Lord is the beginning of
knowledge,
but fools despise wisdom and discipline.

Proverbs 3:1–20

1 My son, do not forget my teaching,
but keep my commands in your heart,
2 for they will prolong your life many years
and bring you prosperity.
3 Let love and faithfulness never leave you;
bind them around your neck,
write them on the tablet of your heart.
4 Then you will win favor and a good name
in the sight of God and man.
5 Trust in the Lord with all your heart
and lean not on your own understanding;
6 in all your ways acknowledge him,
and he will make your paths straight.
7 Do not be wise in your own eyes;
fear the Lord and shun evil.
8 This will bring health to your body
and nourishment to your bones.
9 Honor the Lord with your wealth,
with the firstfruits of all your crops;
10 then your barns will be filled to overflowing,
and your vats will brim over with new wine.

11 My son, do not despise the LORD's discipline
and do not resent his rebuke,
12 because the LORD disciplines those he loves,
as a father the son he delights in.
13 Blessed is the man who finds wisdom,
the man who gains understanding,
14 for she is more profitable than silver
and yields better returns than gold.
15 She is more precious than rubies;
nothing you desire can compare with her.
16 Long life is in her right hand;
in her left hand are riches and honor.
17 Her ways are pleasant ways,
and all her paths are peace.
18 She is a tree of life to those who embrace her;
those who lay hold of her will be blessed.
19 By wisdom the LORD laid the earth's foundations,
by understanding he set the heavens in place;
20 by his knowledge the deeps were divided,
and the clouds let drop the dew.

The Place to Begin (1:7)

The Book of Proverbs begins with a statement of purpose (Prov. 1:2–6). All followers of the one true God—Yahweh—would do well to read it. After outlining his purpose, the compiler of Proverbs moved immediately into the basic foundation for all learning, discipline, understanding, and wisdom.

Some have called Proverbs 1:7 the "motto" of the entire book. Without this verse, everything else in the book would be little more than mere human wisdom. Solomon, the stated author of this section of Proverbs (1:1), found that all knowledge, wisdom, and discipline are bound up in a single, very important principle—namely, starting one's life with a healthy "fear of the LORD."

The phrase "fear of the LORD" occurs eleven times[1] in Proverbs, and three other times[2] similar phrasing appears. One can easily conclude that this is a central concept for Proverbs.

What constitutes a healthy "fear of the LORD"? Certainly it includes deep respect, honor, trust in all circumstances, worship, adoration, obedience, and service. Yet, the word "fear" also means that one needs to feel unworthy of being in the presence of the magnitude, majesty, holiness, and intelligence of God. One does not meet God and casually dialogue with him. Some who encountered God in the Old Testament hid their eyes, others fell on their faces, and at least one dared not to speak until his lips were cleansed with burning coals. The Apostle John had walked with the earthly manifestation of God in Jesus, but on seeing him glorified in a vision on the Isle of Patmos, he fell on his face in the presence of Christ (Revelation 1:17). Genuine fear is in order, along with

What constitutes a healthy "fear of the LORD"?

all the other words mentioned in this paragraph for "fear of the LORD."

The next word to understand is "knowledge." In this case, it is a synonym for wisdom. One arrives at that conclusion because of the nature of Hebrew poetry (see the small article, "Hebrew Poetry and Parallelism," in lesson one). The second line in verse 7 is an example of antithetical parallelism, meaning that its meaning is the opposite of the first line. Fools do the opposite of those who fear the Lord. Foolish people fail to base their lives on a deep respect for and healthy fear of God.

Foolish people fail to base their lives on a deep respect for and healthy fear of God.

Wisdom in Relationship with God and Others (3:1–4)

Proverbs 1—9, the first unit in the Book of Proverbs, contains lengthier instructions on various subjects than the rest of the book. Consequently, these chapters are foundational thoughts on true wisdom.

The promise of long life and prosperity (3:2) is made because if one makes life decisions based on the wisdom that comes from God, each child of God will be happier and enjoy the fruit of good choices. The foolish ignore God. They decide on occupations, marriages, the rearing of children, the choice of friendships, places to live, and a myriad of other activities without any thought that God has a better plan for them. In the end, these foolish people find that wealth, success, fame, beauty, shortcuts to happiness, and the accumulation of material things leave them empty.

Verses 3–4 shine as brightly as noonday sun among the instructions on wise living. The two qualities of authentic "love" and consistent "faithfulness" will put one in high standing with God and others. These two words are often used in other places in the Hebrew text as qualities of God himself.

The encouragement to make these qualities into a neck chain or to write them on the heart is not an endorsement of phylacteries as God had instructed earlier in reference to the law (Deuteronomy 6:8–9). Instead, this is Hebrew poetry. It is to be interpreted figuratively. The idea is that these qualities are to become foundational in one's conduct and attitudes toward God and one's fellow human beings. Wearing a cross around one's neck is not nearly as important as behaving in a Christian manner in daily thoughts and conduct.

One who practices morality based on the teachings of God avoids many mental and physical pitfalls of the foolish.

The result of one's personality being grounded in love and dependability is that a person will find respect with humankind and with God. Furthermore, one's reputation as a kind, considerate, loving, and responsible person will grow into a good name. As you ground your own life in love and dependability, when others speak your name, they will think positively about you.

The Polar Star of Godly Wisdom (3:5–8)

The follower of Yahweh will have no loyalty that supersedes devotion to God. The best disciples have learned the wisdom of putting full confidence in God. Proverbs 3:5–6 are reminiscent of the words of Christ in Mark 12:30—"Love the Lord your God with all your heart and with all your soul and with all your mind and with all your strength." Jesus called this the greatest of all commandments. God is foundational to wise living.

Trust is to be placed in God regardless of how circumstances appear to be unfolding. Leaning on human understanding—your own or anyone else's—is a fatal error. None of us knows all about life and how to best deal with all that life brings to us. Do not trust in yourself or anyone else to give you all of life's answers. There are many false guides. Real wisdom is trusting God, who knows all of your life and everyone else's life. By following this well-known text, many a follower of God has found that God indeed makes one's path straight.

God is foundational to wise living.

Go to God as your first avenue of resolving life's difficulties. Do not wait. Trying to work things out for yourself or basing what you do on the counsel of some friend causes delay and often makes the matter worse. In my ministry, I often saw people for counseling after bitter words, unthinkable conduct, or foolish remedies had occurred.

Verses 7–8 echo the previous two verses with a word of caution. Following the principle of trusting in the Lord and acknowledging him in everything one tries to do also brings a healthier lifestyle both physically and emotionally. One who practices morality based on the teachings of God avoids many mental and physical pitfalls of the foolish. More and more we are seeing where certain habits of immoral living cause serious health and emotional problems.

Wise followers of God honor him with their wealth.

Wisdom in Financial Matters (3:9–10)

Wise followers of God honor him with their wealth. The gifts given to God are a symbol of appreciation for God's blessing. A gift given out of obligation is not a gift; it is a payment. Little joy accompanies such a gift.

A disciple of the Lord willingly gives to God's church and enjoys sharing in the church's many ministries. Meager giving begets meager blessing. Cheerful giving results in a bountiful blessing.

This passage indicates that if one gives to the Lord, God will return many physical returns—"barns will be filled to overflowing, and your vats will brim over with new wine." That is certainly true on many occasions. However, at this point one must apply the rules of interpretation for Hebrew poetry and proverbs. The proverb is better understood as a general truth, and not a literal truth. One is not guaranteed financial wealth merely by giving a sacrifice. If that were true, then Wall Street would be out of business, because giving money to some godly church or organization would always bring guaranteed material wealth. Most thinking Christians know this is not true.

One gives out of love, appreciation, devotion, and worship.

Instead, the principle in this proverb is that a well-meant sacrifice to God will result in God's blessings in many wonderful ways. At times this blessing will include financial blessings. On other occasions, the blessings may not be physical at all. In either case, a disciple does not give to God in order to receive. One gives out of love, appreciation, devotion, and worship.

Wisdom in Receiving the Lord's Discipline (3:11–12)

The word "discipline" in English has changed in meaning from the Latin word *disciplina*. The Latin word originally meant *to teach*. "Discipline" can certainly be punishment, but it is better understood in the Latin origin of the word. Thus, the first purpose of discipline is to teach the one being disciplined some lesson of life.

With that understanding, consider "the LORD's discipline" in this passage. God is not a harsh, unmerciful father. However, like all loving fathers, God lovingly seeks to teach us a lesson about life. There is a twofold warning here. We are not to "despise"[3] the Lord's discipline or "resent"[4] his rebuke. Some hold that a loving God does not punish or discipline people. These well-intentioned people want to preserve God's reputation as benevolent and endlessly tolerant. That is not the God of the Bible. There are times when God's patience comes to an end and God inflicts measured discipline on his children. The Lord did so in numerous cases relating to Israel as well as to various individuals.

> *Trust the Lord, and do not rely on human wisdom.*

God does not lose his temper and inflict punishment in a fit of rage. Rather, God lovingly measures out an appropriate lesson to teach us to return to the wise ways of fearing the Lord and leaning not on our own counsel and knowledge. God is a loving Father and never wishes to devastate his child.

Summary of the Virtues of Wisdom (3:13–20)

In this passage, "wisdom" is personified. That is, "wisdom" has personality and desirable qualities. Wisdom is described in metaphors of high value. Note that the image of wisdom in these verses is feminine. Her qualities make her very desirable—more valuable than silver, gold, or rubies. She offers long life, riches, and honor, and she provides happiness and peace. In every way, godly wisdom is attractive. Embracing her will bring a life of joy.

By means of this same kind of wisdom, God created the heavens and the earth (Prov. 3:19–20). God's infallible wisdom set the universe in motion. The universe is unfolding according to a grand divine plan. Many mysteries about our physical world still await discovery by humankind.

Since we are a part of creation, God has a plan for us based on his wisdom. In what may seem to be a world out of control, the disciple of Yahweh puts trust and full confidence in God, who is in charge. Although we may not understand things fully and clearly now, a time is coming when we shall see God face to face and all things will be made clear to us. Trust the Lord, and do not rely on human wisdom.

Wisdom Literature

In order to understand Proverbs, one must understand some principles of biblical interpretation. Biblical literature comes in various literary forms. Prose (or narrative), poetry, prophecy, apocalyptic, parable, and wisdom are some of the types of literature found in the Bible.

Naturally, one would not interpret poetic literature in the same fashion one would interpret narrative literature. Narrative is the most common type of literature in the Bible and can usually be understood literally. Poetry is the second most common literary form in the Bible and usually should be interpreted figuratively.

The Book of Proverbs is both poetry and wisdom literature. Therefore, one should not approach the teachings of Proverbs with a literal and exacting mindset. One will be disappointed if one expects literal fulfillment every time a proverb is applied. The various proverbs are not rules that guarantee an exact payback for following them literally. Instead, these are principles of attitude and behavior that when applied can provide a happier and more godly lifestyle.

Questions

1. Which biblical proverbs guide your life?

2. Do you believe that most Christians exhibit a healthy "fear of the Lord"? Give reasons for your answer.

3. Do most of the Christians in your church practice authentic love and genuine kindness toward one another? Have you ever been in a church in which most members did not practice these two attributes?

4. What mistakes have you seen people make because they did not seek God's plan for their lives?

5. What are some differences between biblical wisdom and human knowledge that does not rely on God?

NOTES

1. Proverbs 1:7; 2:5; 9:10; 10:27; 14:27; 15:16, 33; 16:6; 19:23; 22:4; 23:17.
2. Proverbs 1:29; 8:13; 14:26.
3. The Hebrew word means *reject* or *take lightly.*
4. The Hebrew word means *loathe* or *abhor.*

LESSON ELEVEN Wisdom for Right Living

Focal Text

Proverbs 11:1–11, 17–21, 23–25, 28

Background

Proverbs 10:1—22:16

Main Idea

Wise people practice righteousness.

Question to Explore

How does wisdom express itself in life?

Study Aim

To identify the actions, attitudes, and results of right living

Study and Action Emphases

- Affirm the Bible as our authoritative guide for life and ministry
- Develop a growing, vibrant faith
- Obey and serve Jesus by meeting physical, spiritual, and emotional needs
- Equip people for servant leadership

Quick Read

Righteousness provides benefits in all walks of daily life. Righteousness is doing what is right according to God's—not people's—standard.

Where did you learn right from wrong? As I look back over my life, I learned most about the difference between right and wrong from my parents in my formative years. Certainly others contributed as I grew older and my world began to expand. Yet, it was my mom and dad who taught me proper, acceptable conduct.

I never heard a single swear word or any ungodly conversation from either of them. Furthermore, they tolerated no foul language. I had my mouth washed out with soap if I uttered a foul word. Although having my mouth washed out with soap was an unpleasant experience and extremely distasteful, it afforded no lasting damage on my psyche or to my physical body. It was a great deterrent to using unacceptable language.

My parents practiced what they preached. My dad was no different outside the home from the person he was in our home. He detested lying, and I cannot think of a single time when I thought he lied about anything.

My dad was a "man's man." He was intelligent and physically fit. We learned to fish, use a rifle properly, be active in the Scouting program (my mom was a Cub Scout leader), play ball of every kind, know how to use a knife, do yard work—the list is endless. I learned my sex education from my dad when we went fishing. My brother and I were a captive audience in the fishing boat. In the process, my dad taught us a high view of women.

Later, when I headed off to college, my dad gave me this advice: "Son, I have found that when I obeyed the Ten Commandments I was happier, and when I broke the Ten Commandments I was unhappier." That's it! No long drawn-out philosophy. As I look back, my dad was right on target. Every word of that advice has been true in my life also.

My father learned most of his morality from his dad (a Baptist preacher, farmer, and schoolteacher) and from Scripture. He peppered my life with home-spun American proverbs and biblical proverbs straight out of the lesson we have for today.

Proverbs 11:1–11, 17–21, 23–25, 28

1 The LORD abhors dishonest scales,
but accurate weights are his delight.
2 When pride comes, then comes disgrace,
but with humility comes wisdom.
3 The integrity of the upright guides them,
but the unfaithful are destroyed by their
duplicity.
4 Wealth is worthless in the day of wrath,
but righteousness delivers from death.
5 The righteousness of the blameless makes a
straight way for them,
but the wicked are brought down by their own
wickedness.
6 The righteousness of the upright delivers them,
but the unfaithful are trapped by evil desires.

7 When a wicked man dies, his hope perishes;
all he expected from his power comes to
nothing.
8 The righteous man is rescued from trouble,
and it comes on the wicked instead.
9 With his mouth the godless destroys his neighbor,
but through knowledge the righteous escape.
10 When the righteous prosper, the city rejoices;
when the wicked perish, there are shouts of joy.
11 Through the blessing of the upright a city is
exalted,
but by the mouth of the wicked it is destroyed.

17 A kind man benefits himself,
but a cruel man brings trouble on himself.
18 The wicked man earns deceptive wages,
but he who sows righteousness reaps a sure
reward.
19 The truly righteous man attains life,
but he who pursues evil goes to his death.
20 The LORD detests men of perverse heart
but he delights in those whose ways are
blameless.
21 Be sure of this: The wicked will not go
unpunished,
but those who are righteous will go free.

23 The desire of the righteous ends only in good,
but the hope of the wicked only in wrath.
24 One man gives freely, yet gains even more;
another withholds unduly, but comes to
poverty.
25 A generous man will prosper;
he who refreshes others will himself be
refreshed.

• • • • • • • • • • • • • • • • •

28 Whoever trusts in his riches will fall,
but the righteous will thrive like a green leaf.

Employing Godly Righteousness in Daily Life (11:1–11)

Where did you learn right from wrong?

Each verse in this section of Proverbs provides insight into the beneficial results of righteous living. Whereas these verses may seem to be disconnected from one another, all point to some segment of righteous living. Verses 1–4 show the value of moral integrity and the punishment for unethical behavior.

In referring to the Lord in verse 1, the author emphasized that the Lord is as interested in one's behavior in the marketplace as in one's behavior in worship. This verse teaches that honesty is the basis of righteous business practices. Worship that does not carry over into our daily living is useless.

In verse 1, the words translated "dishonest scales" are literally in the Hebrew *balances of deceit. Deceit* carries the idea of deliberate and premeditated attempts of trickery and treachery.

In verses 2–3, the concept of righteous living is continued. Verse 2 encourages humility. Haughtiness, pride, and arrogance lead to dishonor, because God is omitted from such a life. It is difficult to be arrogant when we realize that all we have comes from God. God is the source of human talent, intelligence, material wealth, beauty, health, and wisdom. Realizing this, we should be humble about our abilities and achievements.

Worship that does not carry over into our daily living is useless.

Verse 3 teaches that an upright person lives by his or her honesty. Consistent integrity provides dividends over time. People come to know and rely on one's honest conduct. Consequently, honesty is not a one-time act; rather, it is habitual.

The "day of the LORD" is a frequent phrase throughout the Bible (see Amos 5:18). A day of reckoning is coming. Here in verse 4, the phrase is changed slightly and is stated specifically as a warning. The day of the Lord will be a "day of wrath" for the disobedient and unrighteous.

What value does earthly wealth have in eternal life? Everyone will live eternally. The unrighteous non-believer also lives forever in torment. Our lifetimes are limited to a few earthly years. When one thinks of eternity, a human lifetime is almost insignificant. Why then do we spend so much time accumulating *stuff*? What good is a bank account, house(s), automobiles, education, a stock portfolio, jewelry, clothing, or any other item of wealth and status 10,000 years from now? What really is of value forever? The answer to this question should guide one closer to faith in God and obedience to him.

When one thinks of eternity, a human lifetime is almost insignificant.

Proverbs 11:5–6 forms a proverb pair. Both proverbs are variations on each other. The first, verse 5, teaches the results of righteous and unrighteous living. The second, verse 6, states that evil conduct is a snare. Eventually, one's acts of evil will turn on the perpetrator and destroy him or her. God's justice is fair and a bit ironic in this matter.

The next two verses, verses 7–8, tell of the death of the wicked. Clearly, in many cases it seems that the wicked do very well in life. In many cases, wicked people appear to suffer very little for their lifestyle. Yet, death is a great equalizer. In death, the wicked have no hope. Instead, they face the judgment of God. Christians have a great hope of everlasting joy and reward from God, because our sins are forgiven through the death and resurrection of Jesus Christ. The righteous avoid the trouble that besets the wicked.

Verses 9–11 conclude this section of our study on righteous living and its results. Verse 9 shows the folly of unwise and hurtful conversation. In many places in the Bible, the sins of the tongue and their results are condemned.

I have found that most if not all Christians are guilty of lying at one time or another. Many tend to downplay this terrible and wicked sin, because we ourselves have done it. Let us be clear, though, that lying, gossip, slander, and backbiting are condemned in Scripture.

Verses 10–11 are another example of two proverbs that teach the same lesson. We rejoice when we see someone receive the blessings of good living. We take heart that righteousness is well worth the effort in this life. On the other hand, it is an encouragement to see God's justice visited on the unrighteous in this lifetime. Many were glad when Adolph Hitler perished and no longer threatened the world. Righteous people bless whole communities, and whole communities suffer by unrighteousness, including in speech. The church rejoices over righteous actions and suffers when one or more members act unrighteously.

The Results of Personal Conduct (11:17–21, 23–25, 28)

Both righteous living and wicked living have consequences. Both extract a price. Verse 17 pictures the boomerang effect of good or evil deeds. What a person does in life affects his or her well-being. An individual will feel the results in soul and body.

Note that the word "himself" appears twice in verse 17. Each is from a different Hebrew word. The first occurrence is the word often translated *soul.* The second occurrence is a Hebrew word often translated *flesh.* Thus, the verse implies that kindness is a genuine benefit to an individual's soul. The second part of the verse can be translated, *A cruel man brings trouble upon his flesh.* One meaning is that cruelty generates bad feelings. A cruel person lacks compassion and misses the resultant feeling of having done well by someone. Cruelty would be an uneasy life simply because a cruel person cannot trust others. He or she will wonder whether others will respond in the same way. This verse says we should be kind to all, even to those who are cruel to us.

What a person does in life affects his or her well-being.

Verses 18–19 fit together. Each agrees with the thinking of the other. Verse 18 begins by suggesting that it may seem that wickedness pays off well in this life. It may appear that evil wins over righteousness. Such a notion, though, is deceptive. A truly wise person knows that there is more to life than a physical lifetime. Death is the penalty of sin. For the unrighteous, death results in an everlasting life of torment and anguish whereas righteous conduct reaps heavenly rewards. Good works do not save. Yet, good works are a natural by-product of a saved life. Christ makes a difference. One's pattern for conduct is Jesus.

God detests people with a "perverse heart" (11:20). The image is that the person's thinking and actions are twisted away from godliness. Let us not forget the reality of the judgment of God on a wicked and unrighteous life. Scripture teaches that some actions are an abomination to God. He expresses outrage at the lack of righteousness in a person's thoughts and conduct.

On the other hand, God delights in those whose ways are "blameless." The word "blameless" does not mean *sinless*. Instead, it refers to an upright life. Remember that few of us could stand to be judged by only one event in our lifetime. Yet, that is exactly what many of us do to our fellow Christians. We see a sin in their lives and let it color our viewpoint of them for the rest of their lives.

Generosity breeds happiness, while stinginess breeds contempt.

When I was nineteen years old, I was arrested for disturbing the peace. My friends and I were guilty, and so we pleaded guilty in court. I would hate to be remembered for the foolishness of that one event in my long life. I hope that the decades of Christian service and godly living demonstrate what I really am as compared to what I did more than forty-five years ago. Actually, today I laugh about the folly of that unwise act. Although it was not at all funny when it happened, I know—as do others—that was not the real person I am today. God sees my whole life, not just one incident. He treats you and all others the same way.

Verse 21 was part of the teaching my parents gave to me early in life. We often see what appears to be injustice in this life. People do awful deeds to other people. This verse deals with justice in the divine court of God. We will give an account of ourselves before God for everything we have said and done (2 Corinthians 5:10).

When Idi Amin was cruelly ruling in Uganda in the 1970s, I prayed for the people of that African nation. Amin was persecuting Christians and Jews particularly. With his support, terrorists hijacked an Air France flight carrying many Jewish passengers. The plane landed at Entebbe airport. In a daring raid on July 3–4, 1976, the Israelis flew commandos into the airport and freed the hostages.

Without righteousness, wealth is worthless.

Amin reportedly killed 300,000 Ugandan citizens. One thinks of verse 21, "The wicked will not go unpunished," when pondering the justice of God and the evil things people do. Amin died in 2003. God definitely brings justice, certainly at the end of life.

In verse 23, the writer of Proverbs provides a statement on two kinds of behavior and the results of each. "Desire" in this verse refers to our longings and cravings. Those whose sincere ambition is to act righteously in thought and conduct will eventually reap good rewards for their effort. However, the wicked will reap only the wrath of God in both this life and the next.

Verses 24–25 extol generosity. This generosity is not financial generosity only. Instead, the reference is to all areas of life. There is an unspeakable joy in exercising kindness. Those who practice no mercy or kindness seldom receive mercy or kindness in return. There is a dearth of reward for the stingy. Verse 25 speaks particularly to this concept. When we give love, devotion, appreciation, and hope, our souls receive refreshment. It brings great joy to see others' surprise and delight when we shower them with generous portions of love and kindness. It makes one feel so much better than behaving with bitterness and stinginess. Generosity breeds happiness, while stinginess breeds contempt.

Finally, verse 28 teaches us that security about the future rests with trusting God and living righteously, not in relying on material goods. The righteous trust in God to provide a future life of grand beauty and enormous well-being in heaven. The image used here is that of a "green leaf." In the ancient Near East, this phrase was common in referring to prosperity and fertility. "Green leaf" is a metaphor for being alive and flourishing.

All things being equal, wealth is not evil. Wealth, though, turns into a snare when it comes to us by means of immoral practices or is used for selfish goals. The Bible is highly suspicious of the wealthy. Yet, the

Bible commends those who use wealth to glorify God. Without righteousness, wealth is worthless. Christians who receive material gain should willingly use their financial strength to perform acts that are pleasing to God.

Righteousness

The word *righteousness* appears often in Scripture, and many people misinterpret its true meaning. The word does not carry the idea of sinlessness. Many Christians believe that since they are sinners, righteousness could never be descriptive of their Christian life. They feel like failures.

The word, though, really refers to one's overall lifestyle. Righteousness in Scripture always refers to right conduct according to the commands of God. One lives righteously when one seeks continually to do right in his or her life. Choosing to do what is right in the eyes of God is righteousness.

Case Study

Suppose a member of your church is willing to pay for re-roofing the sanctuary but attaches one condition. (This story actually happened to me in my ministry.) The condition is that the pastor ask people of another race to find another church. The cost of re-roofing is beyond the church's current financial ability and leaks are causing weekly damage to the place of worship. What would you advise the pastor to do and why?

Questions

1. Which of the proverbs in today's lesson means the most to you? Why?

2. In God's sight, are some sins worse than other sins? If so, which ones? Why do you think that?

3. If you received $1 million tax-free today, how would you use it? Why?

LESSON TWELVE

Wisdom for Every Area of Life

Focal Text

Proverbs 22:17–25; 23:10–11, 19–28; 24:10–12, 15–20

Background

Proverbs 22:17—24:22

Main Idea

Wisdom calls for right living in every area of life.

Question to Explore

How does the ancient wisdom of Proverbs apply to modern life?

Study Aim

To identify implications of these proverbs for modern life

Study and Action Emphases

- Affirm the Bible as our authoritative guide for life and ministry
- Share the gospel with all people
- Develop a growing, vibrant faith
- Encourage healthy families
- Obey and serve Jesus by meeting physical, spiritual, and emotional needs
- Equip people for servant leadership

Quick Read

Daily living is helped by reading, studying, and applying the biblical proverbs to our lives.

As a ministerial student in a Baptist college and later in seminary, I was introduced to the fact that many parallels to Scripture appear in other ancient religions and philosophies. At first this startled me and I did not know what to think of this new information. Yet, I had wonderful professors who deeply loved the Bible. They taught me not to be alarmed.

Did the writers of the Bible simply borrow non-biblical literature or sayings and place them in the Bible? Absolutely not! It may be that ancient philosophies borrowed from the biblical writers. Furthermore, the biblical writers wrote under the inspiration of the Holy Spirit to guarantee that only truth would be in the Bible. If and when God led a writer to use or borrow a story, truth, or spiritual idea from secular writers, God also led the biblical writer to revise the material to be true and reliable. The Bible is fully trustworthy and completely inspired by God.

Proverbs 22:17–25

17 Pay attention and listen to the sayings of the wise;
apply your heart to what I teach,
18 for it is pleasing when you keep them in your heart
and have all of them ready on your lips.
19 So that your trust may be in the LORD,
I teach you today, even you.

20 Have I not written thirty sayings for you,
sayings of counsel and knowledge,
21 teaching you true and reliable words,
so that you can give sound answers
to him who sent you?
22 Do not exploit the poor because they are poor
and do not crush the needy in court,
23 for the LORD will take up their case
and will plunder those who plunder them.
24 Do not make friends with a hot-tempered man,
do not associate with one easily angered,
25 or you may learn his ways
and get yourself ensnared.

Proverbs 23:10–11, 19–28

10 Do not move an ancient boundary stone
or encroach on the fields of the fatherless,
11 for their Defender is strong;
he will take up their case against you.

• • • • • • • • • • • • • • • • •

19 Listen, my son, and be wise,
and keep your heart on the right path.
20 Do not join those who drink too much wine
or gorge themselves on meat,
21 for drunkards and gluttons become poor,
and drowsiness clothes them in rags.

22 Listen to your father, who gave you life,
and do not despise your mother when she is old.
23 Buy the truth and do not sell it;
get wisdom, discipline and understanding.
24 The father of a righteous man has great joy;
he who has a wise son delights in him.
25 May your father and mother be glad;
may she who gave you birth rejoice!
26 My son, give me your heart
and let your eyes keep to my ways,
27 for a prostitute is a deep pit
and a wayward wife is a narrow well.
28 Like a bandit she lies in wait,
and multiplies the unfaithful among men.

Proverbs 24:10–12, 15–20

10 If you falter in times of trouble,
how small is your strength!
11 Rescue those being led away to death;
hold back those staggering toward slaughter.
12 If you say, "But we knew nothing about this,"
does not he who weighs the heart perceive it?
Does not he who guards your life know it?
Will he not repay each person according to what he has done?

15 Do not lie in wait like an outlaw against a
righteous man's house,
do not raid his dwelling place;
16 for though a righteous man falls seven times, he
rises again,
but the wicked are brought down by calamity.
17 Do not gloat when your enemy falls;
when he stumbles, do not let your heart rejoice,
18 or the LORD will see and disapprove
and turn his wrath away from him.
19 Do not fret because of evil men
or be envious of the wicked,
20 for the evil man has no future hope,
and the lamp of the wicked will be snuffed out.

The Thirty Sayings of the Wise (22:17—24:22)

To fully appreciate this section of Proverbs, one must give close attention to dramatic changes in the text. Such a change occurs in 22:17. Not only is this a new section of Proverbs, but the style of writing and phrasing changes. There are thirty sayings in this section (Proverbs 22:20). The teachings found here are remarkably similar to the *Instruction of Amenemope* of Egypt.[1] (See the small article, "The Origin of Proverbs," elsewhere in this lesson.)

The thirty "sayings of the wise" (Prov. 22:17) are brief positive or negative precepts that show a person the reasons for being obedient to God. The reader is addressed in the second person, using "you" or "your" frequently. Because the reader is addressed directly, a personal response is expected.

An introduction to the thirty sayings is found in 22:17–21. Note in these verses the purpose of these sayings. One purpose is stated in verse 21: "so that you can give sound answers to him who sent you." This purpose also appears in the *Instruction of Amenemope*. The biblical writer states a more important purpose in verse 19: "So that your trust may be in the LORD."

Treatment of the Poor (22:22–23)

The Bible is filled with instructions about godly treatment of those who are poor. Unfortunately, some people are so wicked they take advantage of the poor. They prey on them because of their language, culture, lack of education, ignorance of local customs, or lack of having someone with power or influence to ensure their safety and see that they receive fair treatment. The poor are often easy targets for those plying some "get rich" scheme. Lotteries, gambling enterprises, unethical investments, and con games prey on the poor, widows/widowers, and the elderly. Some marketing strategies are aimed at those who genuinely need financial help.

Godly truth, wisdom, discipline, and understanding are all well worth the cost.

Many Americans have never experienced real poverty. Because of this, there is a tendency to believe that poverty is the fault of the poor. While this may be true in some cases, it is not true in many cases. For example, a large number of American children have no health care insurance.[2] Their parents may be in jobs that have no health care benefits, and the parents are unable to pay the high cost of health insurance premiums. What are the children and their parents to do? The location of health clinics sometimes is a long distance from the people who need them. Getting to the clinic and waiting to be seen can be an all-day affair.

The Bible is fully trustworthy and completely inspired by God.

If you mistreat the poor, remember that God is their advocate and will bring justice on you. God will judge your criticizing comments and lack of concern.

Dangerous Associations (22:24–25)

These verses refer to the influence wicked people can have on good people. We all know that associating with some people of bad character only rubs off on the good person. Ill-tempered people have a negative impact on everyone around them. Regardless of how much one may try to resist, the tendency is to become critical and mean-spirited back toward them. Their constant barrage of anger soon makes us angry.

Unknowingly, we may take that anger back to our homes and infect our families and friends.

Bad habits and bad character are infectious. They poison the wicked person's associates. Before we realize it, we can begin to think and behave like the wicked friend. Talk, habits, and traits are picked up. Jesus had remarkable ability to keep company with sinners without becoming a sinner.

The Bible is filled with instructions about godly treatment of those who are poor.

Few things cause a parent more anxiety than to see his or her child become friends with unsavory characters. Influence can be good or bad. We need to learn how to absorb noble traits and reject ungodly traits.

Respect for Others' Property (23:10–11)

We now move to the tenth saying in our study of these "thirty sayings." Before studying this saying, read from in your Bible the verses in 22:26 to 23:9 so that you will be aware of sayings three through nine. Since the background passage is too lengthy for study in one class session, the focal passage emphasizes those sayings that seem to have the most immediate application for today or that provide instructions on different topics.

This wisdom maxim is similar to the first saying about the poor. It reflects the same idea that appears in Proverbs 22:28 about moving the ancient boundary.

In chapter 6 of the *Instruction of Amenemope*, the Egyptian philosopher used the word "widow" instead of "the fatherless" (orphans) in a similar instruction. The meaning is the same. Those who take advantage of widows, orphans, or others who have no champion for their protection must remember that God is the poor person's "Defender," and he "is strong."

If you mistreat the poor, remember that God is their advocate and will bring justice on you.

Ancient boundaries were usually stacked stone walls a few feet high. Generally these were the rocks that had been removed from the field in order to allow the seed to grow. Some markers ran the length of the field, while others were set at the corners for a line-of-sight fence from corner to corner. The latter were easily moved during the night. Since God owned the land and gave each Israelite person or family a share (Deuteronomy 19:14), moving the boundary was an offense against God. This text envisions a court battle over the property. God would defend the weaker party—a widow, orphan, or poor person.

Associating with Drunkards and Gluttons (23:19–21)

In verse 19, the reader is called again to careful listening. The precepts that are to be revealed are extremely important to the reader and student.

The failure of the glutton is one of over-indulgence. In this case, it refers to drinking and eating excessively. Gluttony is a sin. Many condemn the alcoholic, but few condemn the gluttonous eater. In North America, sloth and gluttony have been joined together to form an obese society. Gorging oneself on wine or food is wickedness and ungodly behavior. Avoid gluttony—and stop condemning alcoholics and drug abusers until you have stopped overeating.

Troubling times show one's true character.

Furthermore, do not keep company with gluttons, drunkards, or those who use and abuse drugs. Doing so can cause your downfall. Their influence might drag you into bad habits.

Honoring Parents (23:22–25)

Proverbs often speaks of the Ten Commandments and reminds the reader of the obligations God's people have in this covenant with God. This proverb echoes the words of the fifth commandment. We are to show respect and honor toward our parents. Because parents are older and more experienced about life, their wisdom is to be sought and heeded.

Parents receive genuine joy from children who practice godly wisdom. Godly truth, wisdom, discipline, and understanding are all well worth the cost. To acquire godly truth one must study God's word and know God's ways. Doing this requires discipline. A disciplined person sees the goal and proceeds toward it without making side trips. To fully appreciate wisdom and understanding, our goal is to apply these proverbs to our daily lives.

Sexual Purity (23:26–28)

Sexual temptations permeate American society. The definitions of sexual sins are changing in our society because some wish to change God's instructions to suit their own ungodly actions and desires. Yet, God's word remains steadfast about sexual impurity.

The author used the words "prostitute" and "wayward wife." We must acknowledge that both males and females can be the source of sexual temptation, however.

Sexuality is God-given for both procreation and pleasure. However, engaging in premarital or extramarital sex misuses this wonderful gift, which is to be reserved for and experienced within the bounds of marriage.

One who avoids sexual immorality before and during marriage is a truly wise person.

Homes are destroyed by sexual unfaithfulness. Sexual encounters outside of marriage strike at the very heart of a marriage. Sexuality is personal and intimate. One who avoids sexual immorality before and during marriage is a truly wise person.

Difficult Times (24:10–12)

Troubling times show one's true character. In Hebrew, a play on words appears in this passage. The word for "trouble" is *sara*, and the word for "small" is *sar*—one Hebrew vowel difference. So the question verse 10 presents is, *Are you small (weak) in troubling times?* Troubling times, not good times, test your Christianity. Do you blame others for your troubles? Do you blame God? Do you question God's character in allowing bad things to happen to you? A truly wise Christian knows that terrible trouble can happen to anyone. It is part of life. The test is in how one responds to trouble.

Failure to act puts us under the judgment of God.

Verse 11 begins with the imperative in Hebrew. So this instruction is a command, not a suggestion. When we see a person in physical peril, we have a duty to try to help. We are not to be casual bystanders. Human need exceeds our prejudices, excuses, or feigned ignorance about the right course of action. We are to act on behalf of the one in peril. Failure to act puts us under the judgment of God.

Do Not Harm the Righteous (24:15–16)

Those who attack or try to seduce a righteous person will receive God's retribution. However, when wicked people fall into sin, they experience no desire to leave or get out of it. Often they see nothing wrong with the sin. Consequently, they suffer the consequences of their bad behavior.

Treatment of an Enemy (24:17–18)

When our enemies suffer under God's judgment, we must not rejoice or gloat. God does not enjoy punishing people made in his image. God does not delight in seeing people go to hell. It is his desire that all would repent and come to him by faith.

When our enemies suffer under God's judgment, we must not rejoice or gloat.

Gloating over an enemy's calamity is ungodly behavior. This passage warns that God may cease your enemy's punishment if you gloat.

Envying Wickedness (24:19–20)

The word translated "fret" in this passage is really a stronger Hebrew word. The first line of verse 19 is better translated, *Do not get burned up*. Some people are angry that the wicked prosper or seem to get past God's justice in this life. Others wish they could live such wicked lives and get by with it.

This passage reminds us that the wicked are ultimately doomed. Their outcome is eternal punishment.

They have no future. They are without hope. Becoming infuriated or jealous that they appear to be living without judgment shows a lack of perception. Judgment is coming.

The Origin of Proverbs

Many of the proverbs in the Book of Proverbs have parallels in ancient Egyptian and Mesopotamian literature. Did the Book of Proverbs influence the writers in other lands, or was the Book of Proverbs influenced by them?

Such discussions often prove fruitless simply because there is no way of knowing for certain. However, for those who believe that the whole Bible is the authoritative, divinely inspired word of God, it makes little difference. If it is in the Bible, it is from God.

Questions

1. How do you feel about the comments of the lesson writer about gluttony? Explain your response.

2. In your experience, do people with bad habits influence their associates?

3. How are the definitions of sexual sins changing in our society?

4. How do you respond when a normally righteous person in your church falls into a sin? What should the church do?

5. How do you respond when a wicked person falls under the judgment and justice of God? How should a church respond?

NOTES

1. The *Instruction of Amenemope* dates from about 1300 to 1075 B.C.
2. In 2004, about nine percent of children under age 18 had no health insurance coverage, according to the National Center for Health Statistics.

Focal Text

Proverbs 25:11–23; 26:18–28

Background

Proverbs 25—31

Main Idea

Wisdom enables a person to learn and practice ways of relating positively to other people.

Question to Explore

What are some practical ways for developing and maintaining positive human relationships?

LESSON THIRTEEN

Wisdom in Human Relationships

Study Aim

To identify practical applications from these proverbs for developing and maintaining positive human relationships

Study and Action Emphases

- Affirm the Bible as our authoritative guide for life and ministry
- Develop a growing, vibrant faith
- Equip people for servant leadership

Quick Read

By studying these proverbs and applying them in our lives, we can become wiser in how we relate to other people.

How do you think those who knew you in high school remember you? How we behaved in those days may well be how our fellow classmates think of us today. A high school student with a bad reputation may carry that reputation until the next time you see him or her later in life.

Likewise, people will remember you today by how you behave. If you show kindness, wisdom, mercy, compassion, and a happy countenance, then that is how people will think of you. In performing a person's funeral, I always ask the family to tell me about the deceased. Many times, I know the deceased person, but never as well as family or close friends did.

Sometimes the family will reveal a bad personality trait and hastily add, *Don't say that in your remarks, please. We want this service to be positive.* I have seen some family members struggle to find positive traits about their family member.

This lesson is about how you should behave toward other people. As you read the text and ponder its meaning, try to find ways in which you can apply each proverb to your life. By putting these proverbs to work in your life, you will build a good reputation for yourself.

Proverbs 25:11–23

11 A word aptly spoken
is like apples of gold in settings of silver.

12 Like an earring of gold or an ornament of fine
gold
is a wise man's rebuke to a listening ear.
13 Like the coolness of snow at harvest time
is a trustworthy messenger to those who send
him;
he refreshes the spirit of his masters.
14 Like clouds and wind without rain
is a man who boasts of gifts he does not give.
15 Through patience a ruler can be persuaded,
and a gentle tongue can break a bone.
16 If you find honey, eat just enough—
too much of it, and you will vomit.
17 Seldom set foot in your neighbor's house—
too much of you, and he will hate you.
18 Like a club or a sword or a sharp arrow
is the man who gives false testimony against his
neighbor.
19 Like a bad tooth or a lame foot
is reliance on the unfaithful in times of trouble.
20 Like one who takes away a garment on a cold day,
or like vinegar poured on soda,
is one who sings songs to a heavy heart.
21 If your enemy is hungry, give him food to eat;
if he is thirsty, give him water to drink.
22 In doing this, you will heap burning coals on his
head,
and the LORD will reward you.
23 As a north wind brings rain,
so a sly tongue brings angry looks.

Proverbs 26:18–28

18 Like a madman shooting
firebrands or deadly arrows
19 is a man who deceives his neighbor
and says, "I was only joking!"
20 Without wood a fire goes out;
without gossip a quarrel dies down.
21 As charcoal to embers and as wood to fire,
so is a quarrelsome man for kindling strife.
22 The words of a gossip are like choice morsels;
they go down to a man's inmost parts.
23 Like a coating of glaze over earthenware
are fervent lips with an evil heart.
24 A malicious man disguises himself with his lips,
but in his heart he harbors deceit.
25 Though his speech is charming, do not believe
him,
for seven abominations fill his heart.
26 His malice may be concealed by deception,
but his wickedness will be exposed in the
assembly.
27 If a man digs a pit, he will fall into it;
if a man rolls a stone, it will roll back on him.
28 A lying tongue hates those it hurts,
and a flattering mouth works ruin.

The Value of Wise Words (25:11–12)

This passage interweaves two separate proverbs into metaphors involving expensive jewelry and wise words. Verse 11 encourages choosing one's words wisely. There is a time to speak up and make your thoughts known. However, caution must prevail. A word or thought at just the right time is refreshing. The gentle word of instruction given when you see a person struggling with a problem is welcome indeed. It is like apples made of gold in a silver setting, suggesting a beautiful and expensive piece of jewelry.

A word or thought at just the right time is refreshing.

The next verse is quite similar. No one enjoys a rebuke. However, when we have tried many ways to solve a problem, it is easy to become frustrated. A kind word from a spouse, parent, or dear friend encouraging us to relax, step back, and get a fresh start is exactly what we need.

Reliable and Unreliable People (25:13–14)

Both proverbs in this couplet use weather similes. According to verse 13, a faithful messenger who aids his master in a troubling time by carrying an accurate statement either to his master or to an associate of the master is very valuable. The picture is of the cool refreshment of snow being offered to people engaged in hard work on a hot day.

Verse 14 affirms reliable people, people who keep their word, by picturing the disappointing effect of unreliable people. Those who tell the truth accurately are refreshing in any society. We want our associates, family, and friends to tell us the truth. We flourish in accurate knowledge. On the other hand, people may tell part of the truth but not all of it. Others may falsify the truth, and still others avoid the truth. This can happen at work, in the home, at school, or even in the church.

People can be like clouds that are thick and dark, with much wind and the promise of rain for a parched field, and yet the clouds pass by without leaving a single drop. Surely all of us understand what it is like when people promise to do something for us or for our group but never come through. They do not fulfill their vows. Such people are useless. It would have been better if they had never made the promise. They leave disappointment in their wake.

Surely all of us understand what it is like when people promise to do something for us or for our group but never come through.

Influencing Those in Authority (25:15)

Proverbs 25:2–8 deals with how one should behave in the presence of royalty or how royalty should behave. Verse 15 may draw attention back to behavior with royalty.

Many people in our society have authority over us. Whereas we could apply this verse to political leaders with whom we have contact, it is more likely that the reference is broader. The reference may be to various people who at given times may have authority over us—teachers, police, firefighters, airport authorities, community officials, and various kinds of inspectors, to name a few possibilities.

Acting in a rude, pompous, indignant, petulant, uncooperative, and angry manner seldom if ever produces good results.

Acting in a rude, pompous, indignant, petulant, uncooperative, and angry manner seldom if ever produces good results. On the other hand, kindness, patience, friendliness, and careful conversation can sometimes break down the hardest official. *Brains are better than brawn* in this case.

Moderation Is Best (25:16–17)

Practicing discipline and proper limits in a variety of matters is better than over-indulgence.

I love honey with biscuits, hot tea, or mixed with peanut butter until the peanut butter is creamy. Honey is good. Eating too much honey will make a person sick, though. It is too much sugar for the body. Likewise, we enjoy visits from family and friends. However, such visits can disrupt our normal routine. An interruption that lasts very long or occurs too often can cause frustration. It is better to exercise moderation in all good things, including visits.

Warning About Unfaithful People (25:18–19)

False witnesses are like a deadly weapon; they can wound or destroy a person. It is hard enough to live life righteously without the added pressure of having someone bear false testimony about you or against you. Gossip, meanness, lying, and backbiting are all unwelcome.

Gossip, meanness, lying, and backbiting are all unwelcome.

A person's reputation is a precious attribute. Without our ever having done something wrong, others can accuse us of impure motives or speculate about our conduct. These evil people often tell more about themselves than they tell about another's character.

The false witness is unreliable, like a "bad tooth or a lame foot" (25:19). You never can count on them. They are unstable and untrustworthy.

Insensitivity to Others (25:20)

Insensitivity to a person's tragedy or heartbreak is unwise behavior. Many well-meaning people say foolish things to people who are hurting, because they do not know or understand the reality of the calamity. Deaths, divorce, serious illness, loss of property, loss of a job, or similar life-changing events are not a time for laughter. Such behavior shows insensitivity to the depth of the hurt the person is experiencing.

Offering your love, concern, and availability is better than trying to use clichés to get a person to feel better. This verse tells us to be sensitive to another person's feelings in a time of tragedy.

Conduct Toward Enemies (25:21–23)

Verses 21–22 call on us to be fair, merciful, and civil to our enemies. Jesus gave similar instruction in the Sermon on the Mount (Matthew 5:43–47). Paul quoted this proverb in Romans 12:20. In the Old Testament, Exodus 23:4–5 gives this instruction for treating enemies: "If you come across your enemy's ox or donkey wandering off, be sure to take it back to him. If you see the donkey of someone who hates you fallen down under its load, do not leave it there; be sure you help him with it."

A person's reputation is a precious attribute.

We should treat our enemies humanely—in this instance in Proverbs, by offering food and water. It is a truth—a paradoxical truth—that you can sometimes win your enemy over with kindness.

Perhaps you have no enemies at all or at least you do not know anyone who is your enemy or dislikes you. You are indeed fortunate. However, you may be aware that you have offended someone either knowingly or by accident and that the offended person does not like you. It could be a family member, a former friend, a fellow church member, a business associate, or a former spouse. We are not to act in an ungodly fashion.

We must remember that God does not treat us the way we often treat people who have hurt us or want to harm us. The fact is that all of us have offended God. What if God treated us as we sometimes treat our enemies? Suppose God refused to give us food to eat, water to drink, clothing to wear, a job with which to earn money, good health, or a myriad other blessings simply because we offended him? We need to treat our enemies as God treats every sinner. We need to offer our love and kindness. God does not command us to love our enemies as we love our families or good friends. Rather, we are to love as God loves. We certainly should not be foolish and simply let our guard down so that we can be harmed, but we are asked to be kind when kindness will help resolve a bad situation.

Offering your love, concern, and availability is better than trying to use clichés to get a person to feel better.

You may want to compare translations of verse 23. The general thought seems to be that a "sly" or "backbiting" (NASB, NRSV) tongue will bring bad consequences in response.

Conversation Pitfalls (26:18–28)

The first couplet (26:18–19) calls our attention to someone who tries to cover up or gloss over a foolish comment that hurts like a branding iron or an arrow. Offhanded comments and thoughtless words can bring harm. Attempts to gloss over such comments only make matters worse. We should be cautious in our speech. We can easily hurt another because we did not think through the words we said. Sometimes the hurtful joke is deliberate. The joker intends to deceive and then laugh at the expense of another. Practical jokers beware. It is funnier to laugh with a person and not at them.

. . . God does not treat us the way we often treat people who have hurt us or want to harm us.

No one likes a person who is perpetually quarrelsome (26:20–22). Gossips are unhappy people. Their only joy seems to come from repeating bad reports about others.

Fires die out without fuel. The best way to deal with gossip is to ask oneself, *By repeating this, do I help or harm the person(s) involved?* If it is not helpful—even if it is true—then do not repeat it if it will not help the person. An unwed mother and her family cannot receive help by gossip. Wise Christians can be very helpful to the young woman and her family with wise counsel, prayer, and encouragement.

Proverbs paints a portrait of a liar in 26:23–28. Hypocritical speech attempts to conceal the evil in our lives. We lie to cover up, exaggerate, make ourselves look better than we really are, and sometimes to advance ourselves over others.

Verse 23 is similar to our American proverb, "All that glitters is not gold." The "glaze" on a pot is deceptive. It is shiny, but it adds nothing to the capability of the pot to perform its function.

Verses 24–26 point out how malice can be disguised by what one says. Words can deceive. People may not really be saying what they think or accurately portraying their true motives. They may be smiling while speaking. In their hearts, though, their true plan is to deceive us.

Verse 25 uses the phrase "seven abominations." "Seven" is a perfect number, and "abominations" refers to being *repugnant* and *vulgar*.

A warning appears in the latter part of verse 26. The liar faces disgrace and exposure. God promises justice. Society will find out about the deception.

Offhanded comments and thoughtless words can bring harm.

Verse 27 teaches that results follow actions. The Apostle Paul wrote a similar thought in Galatians 6:7–8, "Do not be deceived: God cannot be mocked. A man reaps what he sows. The one who sows to please his sinful nature, from that nature will reap destruction; the one who sows to please the Spirit, from the Spirit will reap eternal life." We do, indeed, reap what we sow.

The last verse in our text states two truths about lying: (1) lying is a form of hatred; and (2) flattery is a form of lying. This verse is obviously speaking of a lie told against another individual. We have all seen the malicious venom some people can spew out of their mouths like deadly poison. They intend to hurt and destroy. They want to harm another's reputation or cause others to doubt the character of the one about whom the lie speaks. Obviously, this is not Christian behavior. It is ungodly and worldly. Jesus is our example. He would never behave in that fashion. Malicious conversation is not the conversation of a believer in Christ.

Malicious conversation is not the conversation of a believer in Christ.

Secondly, flatterers are foolish, and what they say is meaningless. Remarks that use excessive flattery do not have positive consequences. The word "flattering" in Hebrew means *slick* or *smooth*, with connotations of falsehood. Most of can recognize such flattery. Genuine compliments are always welcome. Only the insecure, though, require compliments on every deed performed.

Solomon and Hezekiah

This section of Proverbs begins in 25:1 and extends to the end of chapter 29. Note in this verse that this section is identified as "more proverbs of Solomon" (see Prov. 1:1; 10:1 for other sections by Solomon). Further, these proverbs were "copied by the men of Hezekiah king of Judah" (25:1). King Hezekiah reigned over Judah about 715–686 B.C. Solomon had ruled undivided Israel more than 200 years before Hezekiah's reign (about 961–922 B.C.).

The reign of Hezekiah was a period of great interest in wisdom literature in Judaism. The proverbs of Solomon were well known among the people and certainly in the king's court. In an effort to preserve as many of these sayings as possible, under the inspiration of the Holy Spirit, "the men of Hezekiah" added chapters 25—29 to the already existing Book of Proverbs.

Questions

1. Can you remember a time when you received an encouraging word in your time of trouble? Likewise, when was the last time you offered encouragement to someone who desperately needed a kind word?

2. Do you treat your enemies as Christ treated his?

3. What do you do when you hear gossip about someone else?

Our Next New Study

(Available for use beginning December 2006)

The Gospel of John: The Word Became Flesh

UNIT ONE. PROLOGUE AND JESUS' PUBLIC MINISTRY

Lesson 1	From Eternity to Here	John 1:1–18, 29–36, 43-45
Lesson 2	Searching for Real Life	John 3:1–16
Lesson 3	Meeting the Savior of the World	John 4:1–30, 39–42
Lesson 4	Honoring the Son	John 5:1–24
Lesson 5	Relying On Our Only Hope	John 6:1-15, 25-35, 48–51, 66–69
Lesson 6	Believing in Jesus as the Resurrection and the Life	John 11:1–13, 17–27, 38–44

UNIT TWO. JESUS' FAREWELL MESSAGE TO HIS DISCIPLES

Lesson 7	Practice Love Beyond the Limits	John 13:1–17, 34–35
Lesson 8	Rest Assured	John 14:1–11, 15–18, 25–27
Lesson 9	Stay United to Jesus	John 15:1–17
Lesson 10	What Jesus Wants for His Followers	John 17

UNIT THREE. JESUS' PASSION AND VICTORY

Additional Resources for Studying the Gospel of John[1]

George R. Beasley-Murray. *John.* Word Biblical Commentary. Volume 36. Waco, Texas: Word Books, Publisher, 1987.

Raymond E. Brown. *The Gospel According to John (I—XII).* Garden City, New York: Doubleday & Company, Inc., 1966.

Raymond E. Brown. *The Gospel According to John (XIII—XXI).* Garden City, New York: Doubleday & Company, Inc., 1970.

F.F. Bruce. *The Gospel of John.* Grand Rapids, Michigan: William B. Eerdmans Publishing Company, 1983.

Gary M. Burge, *The NIV Application Commentary: John.* Grand Rapids, Michigan: Zondervan Publishing House, 2000.

D. A. Carson, *The Farewell Discourse and Final Prayer of Jesus.* Grand Rapids, Michigan: Baker Book House, 1980.

James E. Carter. *John.* Layman's Bible Book Commentary. Volume 18. Nashville: Broadman Press, 1984.

Herschel H. Hobbs. *The Gospel of John: Invitation to Life.* Nashville, Tennessee: Convention Press, 1988.

William E. Hull. "John." *The Broadman Bible Commentary.* Volume 9. Nashville, Tennessee: Broadman Press, 1970.

Craig S. Keener. *The Gospel of John: A Commentary.* Two volumes. Peabody, Massachusetts: Hendrickson Publishers, 2003.

Lesslie Newbigin. *The Light Has Come: An Exposition of the Fourth Gospel.* Grand Rapids, Michigan: William B. Eerdmans Publishing Company, 1982.

Gail R. O'Day. "The Gospel of John." *The New Interpreter's Bible.* Volume IX. Nashville, Tennessee: Abingdon Press, 1995.

NOTES

1. Listing a book does not imply full agreement by the writers or BAPTISTWAY PRESS® with all of its comments.

How to Order More Bible Study Materials

It's easy! Just fill in the following information. For additional Bible study materials, see www.baptistwaypress.org or get a complete order form of available materials by calling 1-866-249-1799 or e-mailing baptistway@bgct.org.

Title of item	Price	Quantity	Cost
This Issue:			
Psalms and Proverbs: Songs and Sayings of Faith—Study Guide	$2.75	______	______
Psalms and Proverbs: Songs and Sayings of Faith—Large Print Study Guide	$2.85	______	______
Psalms and Proverbs: Songs and Sayings of Faith—Teaching Guide	$3.25	______	______
Additional Issues Available:			
Genesis 12–50: Family Matters—Study Guide	$1.95	______	______
Genesis 12–50: Family Matters—Large Print Study Guide	$1.95	______	______
Genesis 12–50: Family Matters—Teaching Guide	$2.45	______	______
Exodus: Freed to Follow God—Study Guide	$2.35	______	______
Exodus: Freed to Follow God—Large Print Study Guide	$2.35	______	______
Exodus: Freed to Follow God—Teaching Guide	$2.95	______	______
Leviticus, Numbers, Deuteronomy—Study Guide	$2.35	______	______
Leviticus, Numbers, Deuteronomy—Large Print Study Guide	$2.35	______	______
Leviticus, Numbers, Deuteronomy—Teaching Guide	$2.95	______	______
Joshua and Judges—Study Guide	$2.35	______	______
Joshua and Judges—Large Print Study Guide	$2.35	______	______
Joshua and Judges—Teaching Guide	$2.95	______	______
1 and 2 Samuel—Study Guide	$2.35	______	______
1 and 2 Samuel—Large Print Study Guide	$2.35	______	______
1 and 2 Samuel—Teaching Guide	$2.95	______	______
Matthew: Jesus' Teachings—Study Guide	$2.35	______	______
Matthew: Jesus' Teachings—Large Print Study Guide	$2.35	______	______
Matthew: Jesus' Teachings—Teaching Guide	$2.95	______	______
Jesus in the Gospel of Mark—Study Guide	$1.95	______	______
Jesus in the Gospel of Mark—Large Print Study Guide	$1.95	______	______
Jesus in the Gospel of Mark—Teaching Guide	$2.45	______	______
Luke: Journeying to the Cross—Study Guide	$2.35	______	______
Luke: Journeying to the Cross—Large Print Study Guide	$2.35	______	______
Luke: Journeying to the Cross—Teaching Guide	$2.95	______	______
1 Corinthians—Study Guide	$1.95	______	______
1 Corinthians—Teaching Guide	$2.45	______	______
2 Corinthians: Taking Ministry Personally—Study Guide	$2.35	______	______
2 Corinthians: Taking Ministry Personally—Large Print Study Guide	$2.35	______	______
2 Corinthians: Taking Ministry Personally—Teaching Guide	$2.95	______	______
1, 2 Timothy, Titus, Philemon—Study Guide	$2.75	______	______
1, 2 Timothy, Titus, Philemon—Large Print Study Guide	$2.85	______	______
1, 2 Timothy, Titus, Philemon—Teaching Guide	$3.25	______	______
Hebrews and James—Study Guide	$1.95	______	______
Hebrews and James—Teaching Guide	$2.45	______	______
Revelation—Study Guide	$2.35	______	______
Revelation—Large Print Study Guide	$2.35	______	______
Revelation—Teaching Guide	$2.95	______	______
Coming for use beginning December 2006			
The Gospel of John: The Word Became Flesh—Study Guide	$2.75	______	______
The Gospel of John: The Word Became Flesh—Large Print Study Guide	$2.85	______	______
The Gospel of John: The Word Became Flesh—Teaching Guide	$3.25	______	______

Baptist Doctrine and Heritage			
The Bible—You Can Believe It	$4.95	________	________
The Bible—You Can Believe It—Teaching Guide	$1.95	________	________
Beliefs Important to Baptists			
Beliefs Important to Baptists—Study Guide (one-volume edition; includes all lessons)	$2.35	________	________
Beliefs Important to Baptists—Teaching Guide (one-volume edition; includes all lessons)	$1.95	________	________
Who in the World Are Baptists, Anyway? (one lesson)	$ .45	________	________
Who in the World Are Baptists, Anyway?—Teacher's Edition	$ .55	________	________
Beliefs Important to Baptists: I (four lessons)	$1.35	________	________
Beliefs Important to Baptists: I—Teacher's Edition	$1.75	________	________
Beliefs Important to Baptists: II (four lessons)	$1.35	________	________
Beliefs Important to Baptists: II—Teacher's Edition	$1.75	________	________
Beliefs Important to Baptists: III (four lessons)	$1.35	________	________
Beliefs Important to Baptists: III—Teacher's Edition	$1.75	________	________
For Children			
Let's Explore Baptist Beliefs	$ 3.95	________	________
Let's Explore Baptist Beliefs—Leader's Guide	$ 2.95	________	________

Subtotal	________
Standard Shipping*	
Basic Charge	$6.00
Plus 12% of Subtotal	________
TOTAL	________

*Please allow three weeks for standard delivery. For express shipping service: Call 1–866–249–1799 for information on additional charges.

____
YOUR NAME PHONE

____
YOUR CHURCH DATE ORDERED

____
MAILING ADDRESS

____
CITY STATE ZIP CODE

MAIL this form with your check for the total amount to
BAPTISTWAY PRESS, Baptist General Convention of Texas,
333 North Washington, Dallas, TX 75246–1798
(Make checks to "Baptist Executive Board.")

OR, **FAX** your order anytime to: 214-828-5187, and we will bill you.

OR, **CALL** your order toll-free: 1-866–249–1799 (8:30 a.m.-5:00 p.m., M-F), and we will bill you.

OR, **E-MAIL** your order to our internet e-mail address: baptistway@bgct.org, and we will bill you.

OR, **ORDER ONLINE** at www.baptistwaypress.org.

We look forward to receiving your order! Thank you!